A Fashionable Tour

THROUGH THE GREAT LAKES AND UPPER MISSISSIPPI

A Fashionable Tour

Through the Great Lakes and Upper Mississippi

The 1852 Journal of Juliette Starr Dana

Edited by David T. Dana III

Foreword by Brian Leigh Dunnigan

Wayne State University Press
Detroit

GREAT LAKES BOOKS

*A complete listing of the books in this series
can be found online at http://wsupress.wayne.edu*

Philip P. Mason, Editor
Department of History, Wayne State University

Dr. Charles K. Hyde, Associate Editor
Department of History, Wayne State University

Library of Congress Cataloging-in-Publication Data

Dana, Juliette Starr, 1816–1903.
A fashionable tour through the Great Lakes and upper Mississippi : the 1852 journal of
Juliette Starr Dana / edited by David T. Dana, III.
         p. cm. — (Great Lakes books)
    Includes bibliographical references.
    ISBN 0-8143-3205-6 (alk. paper : pbk.)
    1. Great Lakes Region—Description and travel. 2. Mississippi River Valley—
    Description and travel. 3. Dana, Juliette Starr, 1816–1903—Diaries. 4. Dana,
      Juliette Starr, 1816–1903—Travel—Great Lakes Region. 5. Dana, Juliette
      Starr, 1816–1903—Travel—Mississippi River Valley. I. Dana, David T. II.
    Title. III. Series.
              F551.D35 2004
              917.704—dc22   2004000518

Illustrations from the collections of William L. Clements Library, University of Michigan.
Title page map: "Railroads of the United States" accompanying the U.S. Treasury
Department Report, 1852, from the Library of Congress.

The vices and dangers of society are early revealed to her; as she sees them clearly, she views them without illusion, and braves them without fear; for she is full *of reliance on her own* strength, and her confidence seems to be shared by all around her.

—Alexis de Tocqueville on the American woman,
Democracy in America, 1835

Contents

Preface

*J*uliette Starr Dana wrote her journal in a little five-by-seven-inch unlined notebook labeled, "Tour Through the Great Lakes, & Upper Mississippi, Summer of 1852. Mrs. R. P. Dana, Sister & Son R. S. D." Juliette's writing is neat and level on unnumbered pages. Its grammar and style needed very little editing. She wrote without paragraphs except at a new day's beginning, so I divided the journal into chapters and created paragraphs. Her punctuation marks were dots, dashes, and commas and sometimes were omitted altogether. It was frequently impossible to discern which punctuation she intended to use; for example, dashes where periods go or commas attached to the ends of words. I created commas, semicolons, dashes, or periods where her marks were ambiguous. Where a sentence ended in a dash or where Juliette ran together two sentences, I made a sentence break. She was inconsistent in her capitalization and sometimes it could not be determined whether her letters were meant to be upper- or lowercase. Such inconsistencies remain.

I kept dated or what today would be considered British spellings such as "harbour," "grey," "staid," and words with double letters, like "delightfull," "waggon," and "travellers." The more unusual words or apparently incorrect spellings of words and place names I have noted with "[*sic*]," but if Juliette used them often, as with "incounter," or "shewed," I did not continually repeat the "[*sic*]." The names of vessels have been italicized as is usual today, although Juliette did not do so.

Juliette wrote about the Native and African Americans she observed. Her writing reflected prejudices and habits of her time. Many of the terms she openly used, such as "savage," "squaw," and "coloured," are considered offensive today. I have left such terms so as to be accurate to her writing and to history.

Juliette used abbreviations to refer to her son Richard ("R") and her companion Mrs. Twining ("Mrs. T"). Where these abbreviations occurred I spelled out the names. A few times I added a word or two in brackets to clarify a term. Words in parentheses are Juliette's. In the rare event when Juliette lined out words to correct an error, I omitted the incorrect words. A few lined out words seemed meaningful to her observations; I left them in with the strike through.

The identity of Juliette's traveling companion, Mrs. Twining, is somewhat uncertain. "Sister" on the cover label apparently refers to the traveling companion. There is no mention in any Starr or Dana genealogy identifying a sister to Juliette with the married name Twining. The appellation "Mrs. T" used in the journal seems too formal for a family relationship, nor do the journal references suggest familial intimacy with her. Possibly the cover label was added by someone who guessed at Mrs. Twining's identity. I conclude that Mrs. Twining is not Juliette's sister.

A Rachael Twining and her husband Thomas, high sheriff of Berkshire County, are identified in the *1850 Census Records* of Lenox, Massachusetts, and in William J. Bartlett, *Half Century of Memories of Lenox, Mass., 1841–1891* (n.p.). Juliette owned and rented homes in Lenox throughout her life, and spent much time there during all seasons of the year, and her sister Sarah Starr Lee lived there in the 1850s. Lenox was a small town and sheriffs are generally well known, so it is very likely that Juliette knew Rachael Twining and her husband. Remarks in the journal that Mrs. Twining was tired or wanted to rest suggest that she was older than Juliette. Rachael was fifty-six in 1852. It is reasonably certain that Rachael Twining of Lenox, Massachusetts, is the "Mrs. Twining" of the journal.

I have added footnotes to the journal. Where possible these identify many of the people who are mentioned. Those who are not identified could not be, or were so peripheral that extensive research into their biographies did not seem warranted. Brief historical facts about many of the places the tourists visited are footnoted. Occasionally I included a definition or explanation of some word or reference the author used. These notes are not intended to be the ultimate of historical explanation; I only want to give a brief perspective and context without distracting from the journal or preempting its author's remarks.

ACKNOWLEDGMENTS

Learning local histories and identifying personalities could not have been done without the volunteered time and effort of local historians, curators, and librarians in communities all along Juliette's route. These were: C. Fred Rydholm, historian associated with the Marquette Historical Society; Judge Edward Quinell of the Circuit Court of Michigan; Barry C. James, Curator of Education, Michigan Iron Industry Museum; Eric C. Nordberg, Librarian of the County Historical Collections, Michigan Technological University; Phil Porter, Chief Curator, Mackinac State Historical Parks; Suzette J. Lopez, Librarian of the Marine Collection, Milwaukee Public Library; Joseph W. Rutter, of the Sons and Daughters of Pioneer Rivermen; Edward Hill and Jodi Erickson at the University of Wisconsin–La Crosse, Murphy Library, Special Collections Department; Jack E. Custer of Steamboat Masters and Associates; Britta L. Bloomberg, Historian at the Minnesota Historical Society; Tacie N. Campbell of the Mississippi River Museum, Dubuque, Iowa; and Tracey Roberts, Curator of the Galena/Jo Daviess County Historical Society and Museum. Helping seek photographs were Julian Cox, of the Department of Photographs, J. Paul Getty Museum and Joseph R. Struble at the George Eastman House. Thanks also to Kathi Peterson, Librarian at the La Jolla Athenaeum Music and Arts Library; and the staffs of the New York Historical Society; the New York Public Library; the Georgina Cole Library and the Carlsbad City Library, Carlsbad, California; and the University of California at Irvine, Main Library, Periodicals and Special Collections.

My thanks to Hugh B. Speed IV of Lake Forest, California, for the steamboat illustration that graces the chapter headings. Particular appreciation is also given to Brian Leigh Dunnigan of the William L. Clements Library, University of Michigan, and the editors of Wayne State University Press for their important contributions.

Friends Cornelia B. Gilder, Irene Thompson, Susan Zuccotti, and the late Jean Gruwell helped with research, advice, and suggestions. Anita Lamotte transcribed the original journal. Three of Juliette's five living great-great-grandchildren, Juliette Starr Kopper, Philip Dana Kopper, and "Poo" Dana Putsch helped with family information, photographs, and suggestions. Special personal appreciation goes to my wife, Marcie, for her patient support and assistance. Any errors, omissions, or unwarranted judgments are my responsibility.

Foreword

Pioneer Tourism, the Journal of Juliette Starr Dana

"Dressed & went out to the piazza to view the Falls which are here all in full view in their grandeur & beauty. Sat & looked a long time & went still again & again."

Niagara Falls, the awesome cataract straddling the border between New York State and the province of Ontario, is an attraction so well known today that its very name conjures up the concept of recreational travel, sightseeing, and tourism. A twenty-first-century visitor might express her first impression of the great waterfalls in terms similar to those used by the writer of the short passage above. The words are those of Juliette Starr Dana, a thirty-five-year-old wife and mother who took in the scene "again & again" in July of 1852. Like most tourists today, she was passing through, intent on seeing as much as possible in the time available to her. Mrs. Dana experienced Niagara Falls and many other sights of the Great Lakes region that summer in the course of a remarkable, nine-week journey. Her travels took her from a comfortable New York City home to the wild shores of Lake Superior, the upper reaches of the Mississippi River, and back again.

Juliette Starr Dana did not simply take in the sights that opened before her that summer. She systematically recorded her impressions, not with the camera or video recorder available to tourists of more recent times, but in clear prose and wonderful detail in the pages of a personal journal. Her attention was drawn by much more than the natural and man-made attractions that she encountered. Her observations cover nearly every aspect of travel in her time, from transportation to accommodations, food, people, and their behavior. Mrs. Dana's personal account of her summer tour has been carefully transcribed and edited by one of her descendants for publication here as part of the Great Lakes Books series.

A purely recreational tour of the Great Lakes and upper Midwest was still something out of the ordinary in 1852. Many accounts of the region survive from that time or earlier, but most were written by those who traveled for a wide range of other reasons: exploration, commerce, military duties, boundary surveying, Indian or governmental affairs, promotion of settlement, or settlement itself. The 1830s had witnessed the beginnings of tourism by affluent and adventurous Europeans and Americans, a number of whom undertook their journeys with the intention of sharing their experiences in print. Some—Calvin Colton, George Featherstonhaugh, James Logan, John Kingman, Richard Levinge, George Catlin, for example—saw their accounts published. There were women, as well, among this literary group of travelers—Eliza Steele, Margaret Fuller, Anna Jameson, and Harriet Martineau. Their accounts record the appearance of the developing country and its disappearing wilderness, and they also frequently venture into discussions of American mores and national character for the edification and amusement of an audience of armchair travelers.

The journal of Juliette Starr Dana possesses no such pretensions. It is a purely personal document that was never edited or revised by the author, and there is no evidence that she ever intended to mold her observations into a book. Her journal is, nonetheless, well written, highly readable, and packed with information about the region and travel at that time. Juliette was an outright tourist who decided to spend her summer exploring many of the wild places of which she had no doubt read in some of the published accounts mentioned above.

She was a tourist before such activity became truly fashionable in the Great Lakes region and long before the activity was promoted and supported by railroad and steamship companies and by the many resort hotels that would spring up in the years following the Civil War. Her accommodations were at places never intended to cater to a resort trade. The "miserable, dirty & badly managed affair" in Youngstown, New York, was a typical local hotel and tavern. Hotels in Michigan's copper-mining country were set up for businessmen, officials, and suppliers of the mines. The Mission

House at Mackinac Island had been converted in the 1840s from a former school and dormitory for Indian children and was often overcrowded with travelers of all sorts awaiting the next steamboat. The first purpose-built hotel at Mackinac, the Island House, was not constructed until the year of Mrs. Dana's visit. Juliette arrived at Mackinac and her other destinations at a time when her guides were still Indians, soldiers, miners, businessmen, or local officials, and steamboat travel was at the whim of the random arrival of vessels rather than according to precise timetables. Throughout the journal, one senses the beginnings of service industries intended to support travel and tourism, especially in well-established destinations such as Niagara Falls. But once she passed the more settled shores of the Niagara River and Lake Erie, Juliette was in rougher territory and surely on the cutting edge of her type.

In spite of the fact that Mrs. Dana came early to summer recreation on the Great Lakes, one is struck by the fact that so many of her destinations were already being exploited as attractions by 1852 and had developed at least the kernel of an infrastructure to support tourism. Her journey reads like a virtual catalog of the natural attractions that remain the foundation of the region's popularity. She viewed Niagara Falls and the several lesser cataracts of western New York in the Mohawk Valley and at Rochester. She and her companions cruised all four of the upper lakes where they frequently "could see no land & might easily imagine ourselves at sea." She took in Mackinac Island and its already celebrated natural features, and she enjoyed the scenery of the St. Mary's River, the "Soo" rapids, and the wild and rocky shores of the Keweenaw Peninsula, the Pictured Rocks, and Sleeping Bear Point. In the later part of her tour Mrs. Dana experienced the upper Mississippi River with its dramatic bluffs and bordering prairies. The Falls of St. Anthony were her ultimate goal, and the return trip was enlivened by the gentler scenery of the Ohio River and its own attractions, such as Cave in Rock.

Although these obvious natural wonders would be expected to draw the attention of any traveler, Juliette's interests were much broader, and she went well out of her way to experience other sorts of attractions. She passed through most of the developing cities of the region—Buffalo, Detroit, Chicago, Milwaukee, and St. Louis—as well as the towns and villages that were springing up everywhere. The cities seem to have interested her somewhat less than other sights, and although she saw "pretty towns & farm houses," she also noted that "all new towns are so much alike that one description suffices for all." Nonetheless, her comments add further details to our understanding of the rapidly growing urban areas of the West.

Of greater appeal to her were industrial complexes that might not, at first, be thought points of interest for a well-educated and affluent mid-nineteenth-century woman. Juliette seems to have made special efforts to tour mines and factories. She visited the salt works near Syracuse, New York, and carefully described the machinery and the process of making salt. She was duly impressed by the technological marvels of her day, such as the Erie Canal, with its dramatic series of locks at Lockport, New York, and the brand new suspension bridge spanning the Niagara River. The unfamiliar sensation of crossing the latter left her "thankfull when we arrived safely on terra firma." She toured the arsenal at St. Louis and the workshops where "they were altering the locks of muskets from flint locks to percussion." Mines seem to have been of particular interest, and much of Mrs. Dana's time in the Keweenaw was spent exploring the workings of the copper diggings. She described copper ore being processed at the Phoenix, entered another copper mine in a borrowed coat and hat, and descended the deep shaft of a lead mine at Dubuque, Iowa. She was disappointed only to be able to describe the iron mines near Marquette, Michigan, from a distance. Curiosity led her, as well, to tour the prison at Auburn, New York, where she and her companions paid 25 cents for a tour and were told that "the prisoners not only pay all their expenses by their work, but there is sometimes a surplus of 10,000 dollars a year."

Historical sites held far less interest for her. Perhaps it was because the region still seemed so new, and many places that today attract tourists were still in use for their original purposes. Forts Niagara, Wayne, Mackinac, Brady, and Snelling were still functioning military posts, and Mrs. Dana describes them as such, saying very little about the history that several of them had already accumulated. A few sites of relatively recent events—Brock's Monument at Queenston Heights, Ontario, and the remains of the former Mormon settlement and temple at Nauvoo, Illinois—are described in that context. Other locations relating to more distant events, such as Devil's Hole on the Niagara River, are described less accurately by the use of embroidered local folklore. There were few cultural attractions in the region at the time. The museum at

Niagara Falls, Ontario, was one of the few to draw her interest, and that more for the novelty of assorted captive wild animals, the skeleton of a whale, and "a poodle with but two legs," than for anything more educational.

What Juliette Starr Dana missed in the way of local history and cultural institutions was more than offset by her opportunity to observe and encounter a few of the region's remaining independent groups of Native Americans, a sort of ethnographic tourism unavailable to today's travelers in the region. Some had already assumed a more settled existence, such as the Tuscaroras on their reservation near Niagara Falls. Others, such as the people who came seasonally to Mackinac Island and Sault Ste. Marie, retained more traditional freedom of movement. The upper Mississippi was the most exciting in this respect. It was still very much a frontier in 1852, and there she was able to observe the nomadic bands of Sioux along the banks of the river and even talk with some of them in St. Paul. Curiosity about Native Americans was an important element of her tour, and she noted with excitement early in the trip that her son, Richard, "saw the first Indian at Syracuse."

Juliette Dana was certainly not a passive tourist. Perhaps her greatest adventure was the very fact that she traveled virtually unescorted but for her sixteen-year-old son and an older female companion. This seems not to have been as difficult as one might imagine, and she describes no truly unpleasant or threatening incidents, although she was certainly the regular object of polite attentions by the gentlemen she encountered on her way. She was also physically adventurous and did not balk at undertaking potentially dangerous activities. She climbed the various rickety ladders at Niagara Falls and in St. Louis saw what she described as a "Fandango," apparently an early manifestation of what would, forty years later, come to be called a Ferris wheel. These were tame activities, however, when compared to shooting the Soo rapids in a birchbark canoe or descending a vertical shaft of 125 feet, standing in a bucket, to enter an Iowa lead mine. While exploring the Copper Falls mine in the Keweenaw she remained underground while the miners were blasting and breathed the smoke as it rushed past her up the shaft with "a strong smell of gunpowder." These and many other experiences are remarkable not only for the fact that she had them but that she described all of them in such detail.

Somewhat more mundane, but even more important are Juliette's accounts of transportation and accommodations in 1852. Few writers have described the details and experiences of mid-nineteenth-century travel as well as she. Mrs. Dana utilized nearly every sort of public conveyance, from sailing and steam vessels to horse-drawn buses and stages to the smoky, dirty, dangerous railroad cars that were available in the eastern segments of her trip. She seldom hesitated to register her discomfort or her fears. She was frequently seasick or uncomfortable and does not understate the hazards of travel aboard the steamboats of her time. She tells of snagged and sunken vessels, and on one occasion watched as her boat took aboard the passengers of another that had been holed and was sinking.

Her descriptions of public accommodations are among the most enlightening and amusing passages of the journal. She occupied and described numerous hotel rooms and staterooms, almost always with the critical eye of someone who had certain expectations of comfort and convenience. She had little patience for sloppy service or dirty surroundings. She registered approval of most of the hotels in the larger towns, such as the "very neatly kept" Biddle House in Detroit, which compared favorably to "any of the first class hotels in New York." Other accommodations were less suitable, such as those in Galena, Illinois, where her windows faced a side street and the view was of "the side door of a rum hole & an extensive livery stable." She complained that most western hotels were "dreadfully noisy."

Hotel rooms were generally superior to most accommodations afloat. The stateroom aboard the *Northerner* from Detroit to Mackinac was crowded with three berths and no other furniture and "exceedingly uncomfortable and dirty," and her bottom berth was "about equivalent to sleeping on the floor." Bedbugs and cockroaches drove Mrs. Dana and her companions from their stateroom aboard the *Minnesota* while steaming from Galena to St. Louis. When she complained to the chambermaid the following day, the girl casually informed her that "it was no use to do anything, it would only disturb them & make them wild." Small wonder, then, that on her return to New York she immediately took a cup of tea and finally enjoyed "a good, clean comfortable bed once more."

Juliette Starr Dana was a pioneer tourist to the Great Lakes and the upper Mississippi River, and it is fortunate that she was inspired to keep such an articulate and detailed personal account of her experiences. The survival of this document makes available a colorful and insightful account of a woman's first experience with the region.

Brian Leigh Dunnigan
Curator of Maps
William L. Clements Library
University of Michigan

Introduction

*M*arquis Childs, in *Mighty Mississippi*, wrote that journals, diaries, and letters that convey the wild torrent of energy and hope in nineteenth-century America are not common, but are "to be found as one finds early glass and lusterware."[1] This journal by Juliette Starr Dana is such a lustrous find, for it is unique among travel writings. Her five-by-seven-inch book, every page filled with neat handwriting, relates the experiences of an adventurous woman traveling for pleasure from New York City to Niagara Falls and through the Great Lakes and Upper Mississippi Valley in 1852.

Juliette Starr Dana was a thirty-five-year-old tourist from New York City. Her family was five generations American-born. An urbane and well-to-do wife and mother, she traveled without her husband or other male escort—quite unlike other female contemporaries who wrote about their travels. She wrote not to sell her writing or to promote tourism, investments, land sales, or social causes, but for her own enjoyment.

Modern readers will find her descriptions easy to read, vivid, and spirited. Commenting on mid–nineteenth century descriptions about scenery, Minnesota historians Mark Swanholm and Susan Zeik have written: "Those who wrote accounts of their own . . . [filled] their pages with strained allusions, poetic posturings, and pretensions to deep feeling. . . . [T]heir descriptions sound emotionally bogus."[2] Juliette's journal is different. There is nothing strained, pretentious, or bogus in it. The typical rhapsodizing of mid–nineteenth century descriptive writing is minimal. She wrote about some of the most noted scenic highlights of the Old Northwest with clear, accurate prose. And when appropriate, she was able to convey her own sense of romance.

I

Juliette made this trip at a time when her husband was away; she took the opportunity his absence afforded to enjoy some freedom. At the time, women had started seeking legal and social freedom. The first women's rights convention had been held in New York State two years earlier. All along her journey, Juliette noticed the men: a soldier's "penetrating eye," an Indian's "brawny bare legs," an "exceedingly handsome" ferryman. Men she met—soldiers, lawyers, businessmen, and politicians—were attracted to her. She was a charming conversationalist. Male acquaintances attended to her, saw sights with her, rowed boats for her, ate with her, and argued with her.

Her sixteen-year-old son, Richard Starr Dana, accompanied her. He loved riding and driving horses and hunting birds and small game, and his mother took several opportunities to leave him to his own resources in the north woods. An older acquaintance, Rachael Twining, the fifty-six-year-old wife of Thomas Twining, the former high sheriff of Berkshire County, Massachusetts, accompanied them.

Juliette Starr Dana

Juliette was born in New York City on October 18, 1816, to Sarah Goodwin and Ephriam Starr. She had two older sisters, Sarah and Mary. When Juliette was a baby, her family moved from New York City up the Hudson River to the state capitol, Albany, where she spent her childhood. Her father, the son of a Connecticut dry goods merchant, had graduated from Yale College in 1802, studied law, and become a merchant. His business in Albany included travel down the Ohio and Mississippi rivers, and for a time he was the New York State deputy comptroller. In 1829, when Juliette was thirteen, Ephraim died unexpectedly in Buffalo on his way back from a trip west. Juliette then spent her teenage years in the industrial town of Hudson, New York, situated on the river south of Albany, where her mother had grown up and her grandparents still lived.

On July 22, 1835, nineteen-year-old Juliette Starr married twenty-five-year-old Richard Perkins Dana, an international merchant. One of four sons of a Marblehead, Massachusetts, pastor, Dana had left home as a young man to work on a merchant ship bound for Calcutta. At the time Juliette married him, he had twice traveled to the Orient and back. Juliette and Richard had their first child, Richard Starr, on May 22, 1836. Juliette also gave birth to a daughter, Juliette Henrietta, on January 27, 1838, and to another son, William Starr, on April 20, 1843.

After the first two children were born, Juliette's husband resumed his pattern of world travel. He would stay home for six to ten months and then leave his family to go abroad, not to return for several years. Each time Dana sailed away Juliette could not know whether storm, shipwreck, disease, pirates, or war would keep her from ever seeing him again. Taking enormous personal and financial risks, international merchants like Dana traded their ships' cargoes any time or place there was a profit—furs from Oregon, tea and silk from China, opium from India and Turkey. In spite of the dangers, the "China Trade," at its height in the 1830s and 40s, created enormous fortunes for American merchants and financiers. Dana was reasonably successful at his trade and provided well for his family.

By 1852 Juliette and her three children lived in a new and affluent residential section of New York City, at 112 Fourteenth Street near Union Square. The house was furnished with oriental furniture and art and held a library of English and American literature and travel and history books. The city was crowded, noisy, smoky, growing, and very humid in the summer. Juliette and her children often left New York City to visit her husband's family near Boston, Massachusetts, and her own family in Hudson, New York, and Lenox, in the nearby Berkshire Hills of Massachusetts.

Travel in 1852

In 1852, the country's population was concentrated on the eastern seaboard, but it was spreading westward in relentless flows along the Great Lakes and the Ohio and Mississippi rivers and their tributaries. Everywhere in what is now called the Old Northwest new towns and cities were springing up, and the established forts, missions, and trading posts were becoming ever-larger cities. Some settlers trekked farther on to California and Oregon.

Newspaperman Horace Greeley and other writers who had traveled the Great Lakes and rivers urged people to go west. Entertainers, advertisers, businessmen, politicians, and artists promoted western life; they paraded Native Americans, displayed scenic pictures, and sold mineral samples. They published exaggerated romantic reports about the magnificent scenery, picturesque Indians, inexhaustible game, abundant minerals, and fertile soils. Some steamboat captains in St. Louis and Cincinnati advertised excursions north up the Mississippi to see the "red-men." European immigrants went west to find work as farmers, laborers, and craftsmen. New England businessmen traveled west to pursue investments in steamships, railroads, mines, and real estate. A few guidebooks such as *The Illustrated Hand-Book* first issued in 1848 described sites, routes, distances, and fares into the Old Northwest.

During hot summers, wealthy urbanites on the East Coast who had no intention of moving west left the cities for nearby lakes, waterfalls, spas, and seashores where they were pampered at new hotels. Tourists enjoyed steamboat excursions on the eastern bays and rivers and frequented nearby scenic highlights such as Trenton Falls, Wier's Cave, Virginia's Natural Bridge, and Niagara Falls. For cool fresh air some traveled to New England's White Mountains, Acadia, and Berkshire Hills. Trips by train, steamer, and carriage to these vacation spots were familiar and short.

The well-publicized and spectacular scenery of Niagara Falls, the Great Lakes, and the upper Mississippi appealed to tourists. In the 1830s, George Catlin, painter of Native Americans, had been impressed with the scenery of the Mississippi River up to the Falls of St. Anthony. Catlin wrote: "I leave it for the world to come and gaze . . . for themselves; recommending to them at the same time, to denominate the next 'Fashionable Tour,' a trip to St. Louis; thence by steamer to Rock Island, Galena, Dubuque, Prairie du Chien, Lake Pepin, St. Peters, Fall of St. Anthony, back to Prairie du Chien, from thence to Fort Winnebago, Green Bay, Mackinaw, Sault de St. Mary, Detroit, Buffalo, Niagara, and home."[3]

In February 1854, railroads first reached the Mississippi at Rock Island, Illinois. The following June, partying eastern politicians, writers, journalists, and educators rode the train to the Mississippi and steamed together up the river in seven steamboats, imagining themselves to be pioneer tourists. They returned to promote their venture to the Falls of St. Anthony as, "the most magnificent excursion, in every respect, which has ever taken place in America."[4] A member of this "Grand Excursion of 1854," Catherine

Sedgewick, predicted: "the fashionable tour will be in the track of our happy 'excursion party, to the Falls of St. Anthony.'"[5]

Juliette Starr Dana, her son, and her companion had traveled to the Falls of St. Anthony two years before the Grand Excursion made its acclaimed journey. Juliette saw all the places Catlin named (except Fort Winnebago and Green Bay). In addition she went beyond Sault Ste. Marie to Lake Superior. When she made the tour, no railroads reached the Mississippi River. No ships could steam into Lake Superior.

Most pleasure tours were short, not requiring overnight accommodations en route. But Juliette's party toured for nine weeks and two days. They stayed at well-visited scenic stops such as Niagara Falls and Mackinac Island and in growing cities like Chicago, Detroit, and St. Louis. However, a large portion of their tour encompassed the northern and western fringes of the contiguous United States, populated by soldiers and Native Americans as well as by recent immigrants. Very few women and fewer tourists had visited the upper Mississippi and Lake Superior.

Trips west from East Coast cities were most often made for business or migration, not pleasure. People moved on railroads, steamships, and in horse-drawn carriages or stages, often riding with loads of freight. They usually bought tickets on board. They had to find accommodations as they went along, relying on luck or advertisements and recommendations from strangers. Because each community set its own standard time and any published schedules were unreliable, a traveler could not confidently plan for when a ship or train would arrive or depart.

Railroad design did not feature passenger comfort or safety. When travelers boarded "the cars," they sat on hard seats and rode on rough, uneven, hastily laid track. The trip was jarring and noisy. New 4-4-0 American locomotives with nine-foot driving wheels speeding at thirty to forty miles per hour on winding track occasionally broke down or derailed. Passengers could be choked by tobacco or engine smoke engulfing the cars. Trains served no meals; travelers ate quickly at wayside houses and taverns. Water sellers and news butchers hawked candy, tobacco, and papers in the aisles. Short-line railroads operated independently on separate unconnected tracks.

A few steamboats had been built for passenger travel on the lower four Great Lakes and the East Coast. Some, called "Palace

Steamers," sparkled with rosewood, marble, mirrors, brass, crystal, thick carpets, and plush armchairs. But on the upper Mississippi and on Lake Superior, passengers shared steamboats with cordwood, crates, barrels, animals, and all kinds of frontier supplies, even though the steamboats' saloons might simulate elegance with gilt paint and velvet. Freight contracts governed schedules on the Mississippi; missing a riverboat's departure could leave one stranded for days.

Passenger staterooms on the second deck surrounded the saloon, which was used for dining, drinking, gambling, and dancing. The most luxurious steamboats featured separate ladies cabins. The six-foot-square rooms might include a washstand, but passengers used public toilets. Some of the rooms on the better boats had innerspring mattresses; yet many still had only straw on which a passenger could sleep. Such rooms were considered quite comfortable—in comparison to sitting upright all night in a stagecoach, squeezed in among strangers. The only light came from whale-oil lamps in the saloon or from the traveler's own candles.

Not only were steamboat passenger facilities often meager but also the ride itself was risky. Steam explosions caused half the fatalities and two-thirds of the nonfatal casualties on all steamboats. Oil lamps, stoves, engines, candles, and lightning could easily start fires on the wooden vessels. On the Great Lakes, fog caused collisions, and dangerous storms unexpectedly appeared. On the rivers, snags, rocks, and sandbars invariably stalled the boats. On the upper Mississippi, boats collided in darkness, fog, currents, and narrow channels. Of all river steamboats built before mid–nineteenth century about 30 percent were lost in accidents. Some said a steamboat voyage on the Mississippi was far more dangerous than an ocean voyage. During the first seven months of 1852, six hundred lives were lost in steamboat disasters. On August 28, while Juliette's steamer ground onto a Mississippi River sandbank, "after crashing through the trees," the U.S. Congress enacted a passenger steamboat safety bill establishing federal inspection, licensing, and safety standards for boilers, fire prevention, and navigation.

Many of the unpleasant conditions of traveling in the nineteenth century that promoters covered up or Europeans disparaged were commonplace to Americans. Juliette was used to American modes of travel. Following Catlin's "next fashionable tour" itinerary before most anyone else, she and her companions climbed on and off thirteen railroads, fifteen steamships, assorted carriages, stages, flatboats, and ferries. They crossed unbridged rivers and portaged around rapids. To see sights they endured muddy, dusty, and bumpy dirt roads. They covered more than three thousand miles. Juliette and Richard's trip cost $341.62, which Juliette calculated was $2.72 per day each.

There was little that was "fashionable" about such a tour in 1852. But Juliette Starr Dana had pioneered tourist travel to scenic spots that would henceforth draw visitors for decades. For 150 years and on into the twenty-first century, tourists and vacationers have continued to enjoy Niagara Falls, Mackinac Island, Mississippi River steamboat rides, and the woods and shores of Lake Superior.

Notes

1. Marquis Childs, *Mighty Mississippi: Biography of a River* (New Haven, Conn.: Ticknor and Fields, 1982), 77. Childs was a Pulitzer Prize–winning journalist and author.

2. Mark Swanholm and Susan Zeik, "The Tonic of Wilderness: The Golden Age of the 'Fashionable Tour' on the Upper Mississippi," *Historic Fort Snelling Chronicles* 3 (1976): n.p.

3. George Catlin, *North American Indians*, vol. 2: 129–30, quoted in William J. Petersen, *Steamboating on the Upper Mississippi* (New York: Dover, 1968), 249–50.

The term "fashionable tour" can be used sardonically. For example, Juliette's father, Ephriam Starr, wrote in 1818: "a trip to Niagara is now becoming fashionable. That class of citizens, comprising in this country what under an aristocracy would be called the nobility, & who are generally found in our large cities, are always of necessity dupes to fashion. . . . In the summer months, they are tempted to quit the dull monotonous round of dissipation at home, & to roam abroad. . . . Wherever fashion rears her standard, there the birds of their feather will flock, & among the group, the dandys & the cockneys . . . will be seen fluttering in no inferior pride of plumage. In fact a few of these squabs of quality are an important appendage to men of wealth & understanding on the old rule of 'no fools no fun'" (Ephriam Starr to Frederick Norton, November 1818, Dana family papers).

4. *Chicago Tribune*, quoted in Petersen, *Steamboating on the Upper Mississippi*, 285.

5. Catherine Sedgewick, "The Great Excursion to the Falls of St. Anthony," *Putnam's Monthly Magazine*, September 1854.

CHAPTER I

"Worth a Pilgrimage"

JULY 15–JULY 20, NEW YORK STATE

JULY 15TH (THURSDAY) 1852

Left home this morning in company with Mrs. Twining & Richard
S. Dana in the steamer *Reindeer* which left the wharf foot of Murray
street, at Seven O'clock. Had a most delightful day without a cloud.
The boat was a first class one; & well filled with passengers.[1] Passed
the morning in the upper saloon viewing the scenery of the beautiful
Hudson river which never looked more beautiful. In passing West
Point saw a number of cadets bathing in the river. Nothing of note
occurred on the passage & we arrived at Hudson[2] at half past One.

Walked up to Grandma's,[3] & found they had just dined. In a
short time however a very comfortable meal was prepared which
we partook of with the appetites of Ogres, owing to having breakfasted at half past Five & to the keen air of the river. I staid [*sic*] in
the house all the afternoon & evening conversing with Grandma,
Aunts Hannah & Susann; but Richard & Mrs. Twining took a walk
after tea to view the town. Retired at Ten O'clock. Just before step-
ping into bed, heard Uncle Jo's voice whom we had not seen as he
had been out all day.

---

1. Six weeks later, on September 6, 1852, soon after leaving Saugerties wharf on
the way to Albany, one of the *Reindeer*'s steam connection pipes exploded.
Twenty-six passengers lost their lives.
2. Hudson, a "quite large and important" but sooty and bustling industrial city
on the fifty-foot bank above the river's shore ("*The Tourist*" *for 1835, Pocket
Manual for Travellers* [New York: Harper & Bros.], 1834).
3. Susanna Goodwin, age sixty-three.

FRIDAY 16TH

Rose at 6 O'clock & was ready for breakfast at 7 after which & a walk in the old fashioned & neglected garden, we started with Uncle Jo for the cars.[4] Left Hudson at 8 O'clock & arrived at Albany depot at half past 9. While Mrs. Twining was transacting a little business, walked with Richard about the town—bought some crackers & apples to lighten the distance to our next stopping place, & started again in the cars for Little Falls at half past 10.[5] Found we were in the express train, & stopped but twice viz—Schenectady & Fonda. Were but 2 hours & 10 minutes in going 72 miles.

Left the rail-road at Little Falls & dined at the hotel which is well kept & provisioned & after dinner left in the stage for Newport 15 miles distant. Little Falls is so called in distinction from the Cahoes falls near the mouth of the same (Mohawk) river. The river rushes through a narrow gap in the rocks which here almost meet after enclosing for miles the beautiful valley where the carriage road, rail-road, canal & river ran side by side with the most delightful scenery. Got to Uncle William Starr's house in Newport about 5 O'clock & were received most hospitably by Mrs. Starr.[6] He came in soon after & seemed delighted to see us. Talked pleasantly 'till tea and after & retired about half past 9.

SATURDAY 17TH

Slept soundly & rose at 6 O'clock. Breakfasted at 7. After breakfast Uncle William started Richard off with fowling piece, powder & shot to amuse himself as he could. Mrs. Twining sat down to write home; & Uncle & I started on a walk. Went all through the pleasantest part of the village, & saw several pretty houses with pleasant grounds surrounding. Returned & conversed pleasantly 'till dinner. Richard came in—had shot several birds & was in high spirits. Just before tea took quite a long walk through another part of the town & across the covered bridge over the West Canada creek, the same

---

4. The Hudson River Railroad.
5. The Mohawk & Hudson Line.
6. Maria Tucker Starr, age forty-nine. Uncle William Star owned a cheese-producing business.

stream on which 10 miles more to the north are the beautiful
Trenton Falls. Found on our walk a pretty specimen of crystals in
very hard rock for my cabinet. A lady came in to visit who sat about
an hour. Retired a little after 9 O'clock.

SUNDAY 18TH

A beautiful clear day a little cool but pleasant. Staid at home, wrote
to Juliette[7] & Mrs. Woodbury all day with exception of a walk after
tea with Uncle & Aunt Starr. Had no regular dinner but a lunch at
2 O'clock New England fashion. Retired at 9 O'clock.

MONDAY 19TH

Was waked at four O'clock this morning by Richard who got up
early to shoot before breakfast—he killed two birds. Breakfasted &
started at a little after eight in a carriage with a good pair of horses
for Trenton Falls, ten miles off.[8] The day was delightfull with a fine
breeze & the country we passed through diversified & picturesque
in the extreme.

The road for a great part of the way wound with the banks of
the West Canada creek, the waters of which were in many places so
clear that we could distinctly see every pebble on the bottom.
Arrived at the Falls Hotel at half past ten & went immediately
down to the falls. A ticket was given us at the Hotel which we gave
to a man at a gateway at the top of 112 wooden stairs, which landed us in a wild ravine with curious rocks piled in layers to the height
of at least a hundred & fifty feet on both sides, with the river rushing madly & darkly along over an uneven bottom forming foaming
rapids & whirlpools. There are six separate falls, all of them very
beautiful & very different. The winding footpath, in many places,
very dangerous & protected by chains fastened to the rock to which

---

7. Juliette's fourteen-year-old daughter.
8. The Trenton Falls had long been a popular attraction near Utica, New York.
   The West Canada Creek, a tributary of the Mohawk River, flows through a
   hundred-foot-deep gorge in a series of picturesque cataracts, each separately
   named. Fossils have been found in the gorge.

the giddy may cling, follows the stream nearly their whole extent & the rocks seem full of shells of different kinds & other organic remains, of which we obtained fine specimens.

We saw successively Shermans Falls with a descent of 35 feet, Conrads Fall of 20 feet, The High Falls with a perpendicular pitch of 109 feet, which are divided by rifts in the rock into three different & splendid cascades—forming with the chasm, the high banks covered with foliage & the rocky cliffs, a scene of the wildest grandeur. The Mills Dam Falls so called from the regularity & smoothness of the rock, is very beautiful & has a uniform pitch of about 16 feet, with a width of 175. Next come the Cascades with a fall of about 18 feet, which with the overhanging precipices are exceedingly wild & romantically fearful. There is still another fall but we could find no path to progress beyond the Cascades & it is a mile beyond. They extend in all a distance of two miles, with an aggregate fall of 312 feet.

They are worth a pilgrimage through the entire state to see, but the pleasure of the excursion is in a great measure marred by the impositions and extortions of the Hotel, kept at this time by a M. Moore, an excessively vulgar & disagreable [sic] man, & where it is necessary to fee a waiter to pass you anything at table.

At half past three we again entered our carriage & after a truly delightful drive of 15 miles entered Utica through the little village of Deerfield which is one of its suburbs & put up at the American Hotel which possessed the merit of being close to the depot as we intended leaving as soon as practicable. The tea bell rang as we alighted after taking which we (Richard & I) took a walk in the city.

It is beautifully situated on rising ground south of the Mohawk river, & the best view you can obtain of it is from the top of the hill entering it from the north. The [Erie] canal runs through it with handsome bridges over the principle streets. They are constructing a beautiful iron bridge not yet finished over the canal in Genesee Street, the principal business street of the city. As Richard & I passed along, we heard some one saying those are New Yorkers. Richard was quite puzzled to know how they could tell that.

It [Utica] contains about 18000 inhabitants, & is a flourishing & growing place. The Canal is here 70 feet wide & 7 feet deep.

Left Utica at a quarter past eight O'clock in the accommodation train for Syracuse[9] expecting to arrive there at a quarter ~~past~~ before eleven—or in two hours & a half, instead of which we did not get there until Two in the morning owing to the breaking of one of the shafts which move the large wheels of the engine, which detained us in the woods & at Oneida 'till the Express train came up who hitched us on & brought us to our destination.

Drove to the Onondaga Temperance House where we finally got to bed at half past 2 O'clock A.M.

TUESDAY 20TH

Rose & breakfasted at half past eight O'clock. Went to my room & wrote. Took an omnibus about half past ten & went out to Salina to visit the salt works.[10] They cannot be said properly to belong to Salina as they are in every part of Syracuse. Saw the whole process from beginning to end. First we went into a larger stone building where was the powerful machinery that pumps the salt water up from the wells a few yards from Lake Onondaga, to a number of raised sisterns [sic] or more properly houses full from whence they are distributed by large hollow logs to a vast number of large vats where they are evaporated by the sun & air & made into common salt. The finest kind is made by putting the salt water into pans over a large fire & boiling it away—by this process it takes but four hours. There are in our place a large number of shallow square wooden vats where the water is evaporated which have moveable roofs which are drawn over them in case of rain or at night.

Dined & left in the cars[11] for Auburn at half past one. Arrived there at twenty minutes before three, a distance of 26 miles.

Went immediately to the prison & were shewn [sic] all through every part of it by one of the keepers.[12] There are now there 729 prisoners, who were working at all sorts of trades &

---

9. The Syracuse & Utica Railroad.
10. Long ago, Native Americans had discovered the underground brine springs of Onondaga. These springs supplied nearly three hundred acres of vats at the Salinas Salt Works, the largest of America's many salt works.
11. The Auburn & Syracuse Railroad.
12. Prison administrators welcomed visitors. Other penal institutions followed the model discipline system used at this large thirty-five-year-old jail. Auburn

occupations. There are now no women kept there. They are all sent to Sing Sing. The prisoners not only pay all their expenses by their work, but there is sometimes a surplus of 10,000 dollars a year. The keeper said that almost all the crimes proceeded from intemperance. Every Sunday morning they have singing school from eight 'till nine, & then preaching. They all seemed in perfect subordination & very orderly. Everything was as neat and clean as possible. The passages & walls of all the cells are whitewashed once a week. Went from the prison (we paid 25 cents each for viewing it) directly to the depot & at four left for Rochester in what the ticket man called the lightning Express train[13]—where we arrived at a quarter past six O'clock.

Walked to view the falls of the Genesee river in the middle of the town but went to the wrong place & did not see a tenth part of them. Resolved to try again in the morning if we had time. Took tea or rather supper, it was so bountifully supplied with all the substantials & after sitting a little while in the Ladies parlor watching the different trains constantly arriving, retired.

The road today from Syracuse led through some of the richest districts of New York & seemed like a perfect garden with every kind of grain & vegetable in a continued succession as far as the eye could reach. We crossed Cayuga Lake at its upper end where it is over a mile in width & had a more distant view of Canandaigua & Seneca lakes.

Richard saw the first Indian at Syracuse.

---

prison forced inmates to learn trades and to undergo religious lessons to keep them from returning to sin. The admired system also segregated prisoners in solitary cells and inflicted severe corporal punishment. Inmates were forbidden to speak, wore striped suits, and had to march everywhere in lockstep. Tourists could not see the guards lashing prisoners.

13. The Auburn & Rochester Railroad.

CHAPTER 2

"The Mad Tumult"

JULY 21–JULY 23, NIAGARA

WEDNESDAY 21ST

Were called this morning at 5 O'clock & having breakfasted left at half past Six in the cars for Lockport[1]—where we arrived at 9 O'clock & went to the Eagle Hotel where we found neat accommodations & good attendance.[2]

Walked out to see the famous five locks, which give the name to the place. They are double, & boats can go up & down at the same time. The lift of each is 12 feet & they are solidly constructed of hewn stone with iron railings for the convenience of passengers. The deep excavation for the canal at this place is cut through the mountain ridge for three miles at an average depth of 20 feet—in limestone rock. Lockport is 83 miles from Rochester by rail-road. We saw three boats go into the locks & went back by a round-about way to the Hotel.[3]

---

1. In June the new Rochester, Lockport & Niagara Falls Railroad had opened as far as Lockport. The Falls were about twenty miles farther on.
2. Lockport's Eagle Hotel, a log house built in 1832. Over the years travelers had enjoyed its reputation for excellent service and luxurious food and wine. The room cost $1.35. A covered staircase led directly from the Eagle Hotel to the unusual five locks ascending and descending the Erie Canal.
3. That summer Lockport was a bedlam of construction activity. Old strap railroad tracks in town were being demolished. Prisoners were paving the streets with stone. Citizens were building a church, a fire reservoir, blocks of commercial buildings, a livery stable, and extending Canal, Main, and Pine streets.

The day was excessively warm & I remained quietly reading & mending my gloves 'till dinner, which was a very good one & well served. After dinner read again 'till three in "What I Saw in London." At four started for Youngstown in an Omnibus drawn by three horses abreast, and crowded with passengers. At Cambria changed stages & drank a little miserable lemonade. Went on, stopping at several places, through a perfectly level country mostly cleared & under cultivation, with an immense quantity of wheat ready for the sickle & finally arrived at our journey's end about half past seven. Found that our landlady & her daughter were among our fellow travellers. On our way saw a church & several houses built of round stones set in rows with white mortar, in a way that [offered] a very pretty effect.

Youngstown is 22 miles from Lockport, & is situated at the mouth of the Niagara river on the eastern side just below Fort Niagara & is a very uninteresting & stupid place.[4]

The hotel where we stayed is, although the best in the town, a miserable dirty & badly managed affair. We were very tired, & although we knew the accommodations were miserable we had no idea to what extent 'till next morning, when I found I had been bitten all over frightfully, but whether by cockroaches, which were running riot everywhere or some lesser vermin I could not determine. Added to this the sheets were absolutely filthy & had probably served a round dozen men before our arrival. The table cloth & every thing upon it were of the same stamp & took away any appetite completely. Was awoke [sic] in the night by the violence of the wind, which blew down one of the transparencies in the parlor adjoining our bedroom. Got Richard, who had slept with me, to shut some of the windows. There were four in the room—& afterwards was not annoyed again from the same cause. Mrs. Twining slept alone in another room.

---

4. Youngstown was a working commercial port for wheat trade. Drovers, sailors, traders, and ex-soldiers had populated the port for years. From Youngstown smugglers had illegally traded Canadian whiskey and woolen goods for American tobacco and kerosene. The Ghost of Bloody Run, a smuggler in a sheet protecting his favorite spot, had haunted one landing place.

Thursday 22d

As soon as our miserable breakfast was concluded, we started to visit Fort Niagara about three quarters of a mile distant.[5] Our walk was on the high bank of the river all the way & we enjoyed exquisitely the cool breeze which blew off the water. When near the Fort we saw a gentleman of whom we asked the way. He very politely told us & walked on with us telling us he would shew [sic] us the finest view in the world. We found out afterwards that he was Dr. Cattal, surgeon of the regiment garrison here & a very pleasant man. The Inspector General Churchill[6] was expected in a few moments to review the troops & inspect everything.

After the Dr. had shewn us all that was worth seeing, he took us to the Captain's parlor & introduced us to Captain McGown, a Tenneseian[7] [sic] who commands here, & Lieutenants Hudson & Brown,[8] the second of whom was exceedingly handsome in face & figure & reminded me strongly of Blood & the Captain also was a tall handsome man, with very penetrating eyes which make one feel very uncomfortable when they are upon you.

The room was furnished with great attention to comfort, & at the same time in a manner which plainly spoke its peculiar occupancy. For instance, there were snowey muslin curtains & cushioned seats in the windows, & a luxurious couch wide enough for

---

5. The French explorer La Salle first built a fort here in 1679. Later the French built a masonry fortress known as the House of Peace and used it during the French and Indian War, 1754–1759. Battles of the American Revolution and the War of 1812 took place in and around the fort. The American army had built new buildings ten years before Juliette arrived.

6. Brigadier General Sylvester Churchill served as inspector general from 1841 to 1861. He had been appointed General for gallantry and meritorious conduct in the Mexican War, 1847. As the Civil War got under way he retired from the U.S. Army and died December 7, 1862.

7. Captain John Porter McCown, U.S. Military Academy graduate, was recognized for gallantry in the Mexican War. In 1861 he joined the Confederate States Army and rose to the rank of Major General.

8. Edward McKeever Hudson from Connecticut and Lieutenant John A. Brown from Maryland, U.S. Military Academy graduates. On July 3, 1861, Lt. Brown resigned from the U.S. Army and became a Colonel in the Confederate States Army. Lt. Hudson gallantly served the Union Army in the Wilderness campaign for Richmond.

two with ample pillows, but over the pillows on one end was care-lessly thrown a plain sword with a steel scabbard & black leather sword belt, which looked as though it had seen service, as it prob-ably had, as the Captain *had* seen active service, & over the other end was thrown a splendid Leopard skin the full size of the animal. Books, vases, deer's hornes, & natural specimens completed the furniture of the room which commanded a view of the parade & center of the inclosure [*sic*].

While waiting for the General we went to the top of the house & had a splendid view of Lake Ontario, the village & river Niagara, & the surrounding country, & afterwards visited the battlements which also afforded magnificent views.

Now the firing commenced which announced the General. We went back into the house & were provided with seats in an upper latticed balcony, where we had a good view of all the cere-monies.[9]

Before these took place however we were politely handed wine & iced-water, by the coloured servant of the captain & by his order; & had a little pleasant conversation with the handsome Lieutenant, who showed himself both vain & ambitious. After see-ing the soldiers go through all their exercises & talking a little with Mrs. Lieutenant Brown, a pleasant little delicate woman from South Carolina & the only lady there, we took our leave, the polite Doctor escorting us some distance beyond the gate & bringing us the compliments of the General, who, when he heard we were nieces of Colonel Pinkney,[10] said he knew him & would be happy to see us when his duties were over—but we could not wait so walked back to the hotel well pleased with our excursion.

The Fort Niagara stands at the mouth of the Niagara River on the east, & the English Fort George & town of Niagara directly opposite on the Canada shore. There is nothing there of sufficient

9. The house was the much-altered old House of Peace, which served as the officers' quarters and from which Juliette watched the ceremony. The 4th Artillery was then stationed at the Fort.

10. Colonel Joseph Conselyea Pickney of the New York State Militia. Throughout the Civil War he led volunteer units for the Union and by the war's end earned promotions to Brigadier General for faithful and meritori-ous service.

interest to tempt a visit. The Fort is gone to decay & deserted & the town is small & uninteresting.

Left Youngstown at 11 O'clock in the Steamer *Rochester*, a pleasant little boat with music on board, for Lewiston where we arrived at 12 a distance of 7 miles. The river was beautiful of a bright green colour & the banks high steep & highly picturesque. Thought the time very short when we landed on the wharf at Lewiston. Went up to the Frontier Hotel & dined immediately after which we took a carriage on which we placed our baggage & started for the Falls.[11]

Lewiston is situated on the east side of the river just opposite Queenston, which is a small village of no pretension or beauty. Had a fine view of the Queenston hights [*sic*] & General Brock's monument. He was a British officer & fell while leading his men to the battle on this spot. It is a tall column, but the top is broken.

We went first to the Devil's Hole a deep & yawning abyss— 150 feet deep containing about two acres cut out of the steep bank, said to be so called from the circumstance of eight Indians being seen to hide in it in the last war 1812 & although carefully watched for by our soldiers they were never seen or heard of again. The Indians afterwards said that the evil spirit at the bottom took possession of them.

I forgot to mention that we went on our way through the Indian village of Tuscarorra[12] but saw only two poor miserable half civilized specimens of men & two women sewing in a house—one of whom, a young girl very good looking brought out to us a basket of Indian work bags, cushions, etc. We bought each of us an article to remember the time & place.

Our next stopping place was the Chasm Tower on Eagle Cliff.[13] It is 124 feet high & 400 feet above the water ascended by 152 steps & commands a magnificent view of the dark & rapid river, with all the places of note in the neighborhood, with the

---

11. Niagara Falls had become a tourist destination as early as the 1810s. Before the railroads crossed New York State most visitors to the falls took a steamboat or schooner from Oswego at the eastern end of Lake Ontario.

12. Tuscarora, a small reservation for remnants of the Iroquois Nation.

13. Entrepreneurs demanded fees for looking at the sights. A look at the Chasm Tower, Devil's Hole, and Whirlpool cost Juliette $2.46.

Lewiston suspension bridge now constructing. We stopped again to view the Whirlpool, where the waters of the river are 15 feet higher in the middle of the stream than at the sides owing to the mad tumult & boiling up of the furious current.[14] The banks on both sides are steep & high with a plain extending off for miles on either side even with their summits. The river is very winding & is most of its course very deep & dark green.

We crossed to the Canada side on the Suspension Bridge[15] & I felt very thankful when we were arrived safely on terra firma. From it you see both the Cataract & the Whirlpool. It is 800 feet long, 40 wide, & 230 above the water. It is supported by 16 wire cables 1,100 feet long & more than 12 inches in circumference. It cost 190,000 dollars.

We proceeded first to the house of the Custom house offices which seemed to be a mere matter of form, as all that seemed to be required was to say we had no contraband articles in our luggage. A delightful road on the edge of the precipice took us to the Clifton house where we alighted about half past four O'clock. Found the house well filled & excellently well kept.

Dressed & went out on the piazza to view the Falls which are here all in full view in their grandeur & beauty. Sat & looked a long time & went still again & again. Wonder how anyone can stay on the American side where none of the hotels are even near the Falls, & every view is obtained by a walk.

Took tea & another long look at the Falls. They are 14 miles above Lake Ontario & 23 below Lake Erie on the New York side. The river slopes for three quarters of a mile above the Falls making a succession of most beautiful rapids, white as snow. Below the Cataract the river is only half a mile wide, & over 300 feet deep.

---

14. The 1852 *Burke's Guide to Niagara Falls* whirlpool description exemplified typical promotion: "turmoil of waters surging and tossing in this green wood embowered cauldron. No living thing can struggle with this angry whirlpool. Destruction surely awaits all that falls within its reach."

15. The first bridge across the Niagara Gorge, a suspended catwalk of eight-foot-wide planks still existed in 1852. John Roebling's famous two-level suspension bridge for trains and carriages was under construction in 1852, to open in 1855. Juliette crossed on the lightly constructed Lewiston & Queenston Suspension Bridge built by Edward W. Serrell in 1851 for pedestrians and carriages. It was damaged by wind in 1855 and collapsed in 1864.

The Cataract is divided in two parts by Goat or Iris Island containing 75 acres. The principal channel is on the western or Canada side & forms the Great Horse-shoe Fall, over which about seven-eighths of the whole is thrown. The eastern channel between Goat Island & the state of New York is again divided by Prospect Island, forming a beautiful cascade. The descent on the American side is 164 feet, & on the Canadian 158. There is a stone tower erected on the rocks on the verge of the precipice, 45 feet high, reached by Terrapin bridge projecting from Goat Island ten feet over the Horse Shoe Fall.

About half past eight went down into the dancing saloon where was a fine band of wind instruments who [*sic*] play every evening. They gave us several fine arias from popular Operas, & afterwards there was dancing 'till ten O'clock.

Left & went into the parlour on the second floor before they ceased. Saw a very curious clock, over the dial of which was a beautiful flowering tree full of different kinds of birds, which sang & jumped about in the most natural manner. One was at a spring of water drinking. They were the real skins stuffed, & it came from the World's Fair, being of French manufacture. Retired about 11 O'clock.

Friday 23d

After breakfast walked to the Museum stopping several times on our way to look at the different views from different points. Bought some minerals from a man who keeps a shanty on the road. Viewed the collection in the Museum building which is very fine, & then went into the yard where are kept some wolves, Owls, a poodle with but two legs, one animal half dog half wolf, more savage than the rest, some sand-cranes who made a dreadful & discordant noise when we looked at them. Some Eagles who gave utterance to singular & ugly screams, & two fine specimens of the Buffalo. In an out building was the skeleton of a whale.

Returning we passed through a very pretty garden beautifully laid out in the English style with hedges, walk, etc. Richard & I walked home. Mrs. Twining rode. I walked alone to the top of the hill behind the house & had a fine view of the Falls & Rapids beyond them. Returned to the hotel & lunched.

Wrote a letter & dined at three. Immediately after rode down to the waters edge over a road cut in the side of the precipice in the manner of roads over the Andes & other mountains, were roed [*sic*] over in a small boat to the rail way which takes you up 150 feet to the summit on the American side. Took a view of the rapids & the town or rather village, which I did not think much of & got into the cars for Buffalo, which did not start 'till half an hour afterward.

At half past six left Niagara Falls village & after a pleasant ride along the river most of the way, arrived at Buffalo about a quarter before eight, a distance of 22 miles. Did not see a great deal of the town, but it seemed to me much like New York, more so than any place I ever visited. It has grown with great rapidity & has now a population of about 18 thousand & is fast increasing.

Heard that there had been several cases of cholera in Buffalo.[16]

---

16. A cholera epidemic spread through the United States from 1849 to 1854. Cholera is a deadly intestinal disease causing severe diarrhea, fever, and chills. No one really knew what caused it or how to treat it effectively. Cholera slowed bridge construction around the Niagara area at this time. In Chicago in 1852, 650 people died. [The editor moved this sentence from its original location following the next sentence.]

CHAPTER 3

"Lost in the Distance"
JULY 23–JULY 28, LAKES ERIE AND HURON, DETROIT

[JULY 23 CONTINUED]

At nine O'clock we started in the *Mayflower* for Detroit on the river of the same name 30 miles from its mouth. This steamer is considered one of the best on the lake & is beautifully fitted up.[1] Took a severe cold from sleeping with the stateroom window open & the wind blew stormy through the night. Lunched before going to bed in the steward's room.

Lake Erie is 250 miles long & when we arose in the morning we could see no land & might easily imagine ourselves at sea. There were vessels constantly to be seen on one side or the other. We arrived [in Detroit] about half past 2 O'clock on—

SATURDAY 24TH

I went to the Biddle House kept by a Mr. Dibble. One of our fellow passengers was a Mr. Parker whom I had frequently met at Mr. Bidwell's, & who formerly lived in Canada. He came here to visit two sons who are in business here. He was very polite & attentive to us on board. Dressed for tea & read. After tea went to see a Panorama of Italy, which did not strike me as particularly correct. Went to bed about ten very tired.

---

1. The new 692-ton Lake Erie steamer *Mayflower* had been launched at Buffalo a few months earlier.

SUNDAY 25TH

Arose this morning quite early but did not breakfast 'till after eight. This house is very neatly kept, & is in all respects equal to any of the first class hotels in New York. I was surprised at the size of Detroit—as at the style of the houses in the principal streets. It has about 22 thousand inhabitants. It was formerly a military post of the French.[2] Wrote all the morning, dined, wrote & afterwards read in the parlour. After tea walked about the parlour with Mrs. Twining & retired between 10 & 11 O'clock.

MONDAY 26TH

Breakfasted at eight & looked over a book of engravings in the parlour. Took a carriage & rode out. First went to Fort Wayne about three miles south of the town on the river.[3] It is not occupied; & everything is in confusion. Repairs were commenced some time since; but last August having exhausted their appropriation, they were discontinued & so it remains at present. There is a moat all around, & 2 sally ports, one toward the river, the other toward the town. When in order it will be a much finer fortification than Fort Niagara.

The river looked beautifully, & in the distance above, we could see Belle Isle dividing the river into two channels, both covered with sails, & boats of different kinds. Directly opposite is the Canadian town of Sandwich. There was a curious old wooden church there near the water which must date back more than a century, & not far from it, a large stone one with a high & imposing tower, which appeared well from the other side of the water. Detroit is 18 miles above the mouth of the Detroit river & 7 below lake St. Clair.

---

2. Detroit was founded in 1701 at the site of a French fort and trading post. In 1852 Michigan's vast copper, iron, and timber resources were beginning to be developed. Detroit, like other Great Lakes' ports, bustled with commerce and settlers.
3. Fort Wayne on the Detroit River between Lakes Erie and Huron was one of several forts named after General Anthony Wayne, who led American troops against the British and later against Native Americans in Illinois and Ohio.

From the Fort we drove through the city to the burying ground, which contains about 80 acres; & is beautifully laid out & planted with trees & flowers. There are some very pretty tombs but it is evidently new. The greater part of the graves seemed to be of little children. We drove through it by winding roads leading over two pretty rustic bridges. We drove past the residence of General Cass,[4] which was very pretty & embowered in trees & vines.

The city is much larger & prettier than I expected; & we returned just in time for dinner much pleased with our drive. Dined, sewed & read a little. Richard came in in a great hurry to take me a drive with a fast little Canadian Pony. We had a fine time & the pony went beautifully. Sewed a little after tea & spent the evening in the parlour. Retired about Ten.

TUESDAY 27TH

Got up at six O'clock & made preparation for departure. Cut Richard's hair, wrote. At Ten went in company with ten or twelve others from the Hotel on board the Steamer *Northerner* for Mackinaw.[5] All the best accommodations were taken by those who came on in her from Cleveland. It was crowded & we were obliged to put up with one state room with three births [*sic*] for all of us, without looking glass, chair or table. It was exceedingly uncomfortable & dirty.

Detroit appeared beautifully from the water & much larger than I expected. Indeed it has every appearance of a flourishing eastern city, with its water-works, gas-works, machine factories, etc. The seven miles of the Detroit River were very pretty though flat,

4. United States senator Lewis Cass. He had been governor of the Territory of Michigan, soldier, U.S. secretary of war, Indian and international negotiator, and in 1848 Democratic candidate for President. He later became secretary of state under President Buchanan, but resigned in 1860 in disputes over how to avoid civil war.

5. The one-year-old steamer *Northerner* was a 514-ton side-wheel steamboat carrying both freight and passengers. In May, *Northerner* had collided with the brig *Caroline* in the St. Clair River. Less than four years later on April 18, 1856, *Northerner*, loaded with whiskey, collided with the steamer *Forest Queen* and sank with twelve lives lost.

& Lake St Clair a beautiful sheet of water. We did not loose sight of land at all. Sometimes none was visible on one side, but there it would be on the other. The river or straight of St Clair is 35 miles long containing several pretty islands. A good deal of the shore is marshy & all low. The trees on all the lakes so far are small & give no idea of primeval forests.

Just before entering Lake Huron one sees on the American side Fort Gratiot which did not in my eyes look very strong or military although neat & prettily situated.[6]

Directly opposite on the Canada shore is the village of Huron. The shore is very low & the town stands a little back. Next the light house on the American shore, & then we enter Lake Huron which we did late in that afternoon. Lake Huron is 364 miles long.

Four of the coloured waiters of the boat came into the saloon this afternoon & taking four chairs in a row began "a la Christy" to regale our ears with black songs & airs on two violins, a basso & guitar which sounded very well. After it was over a plate was passed around by one of them for contributions.[7]

After tea or rather near nine o'clock in the evening the dining saloon was cleared for a dance. They succeeded in getting up but one cotillion although the musicians (the same as in the afternoon) played several pretty waltzes, schottisches & polkas. It was entirely on too democratic a scale, & although there were many young people on board they did not seem to consider it quite "comme il faut"[8] to dance so "promiscuously." The steward himself took part in the cotillion.

Went to bed a little after ten in the lower birth, which was about equivalent to sleeping on the floor. Slept soundly however, & rose about half past 6 on—

---

6. Small Fort Gratiot at the entrance to Lake Huron was established during the War of 1812 and was abandoned at that war's end. It had reopened in 1828 because of the fighting with Native Americans in Illinois and Wisconsin.
7. "A la Christy" refers to the style of entertainment by the Christy Minstrels, a group of popular musicians in blackface that played at New York's Mechanic's Hall.
8. "What one does." Proper, decent.

WEDNESDAY 28TH

Breakfasted, feeling very funny, & immediately after, after taking a dose of Chollera [*sic*] medicine, which I much needed, went to bed & did not rise again 'till just before dinner at One, dined but was very seasick all day.

The shores of Lake Huron are low with low woods to the very waters edge in most places. As we approached Mackinaw we saw to the north east in the far distance Manitoulin & Drummonds [*sic*] Island. Watched a long time the movements of a large gull who followed us for some distance then sailed off slowly & was lost in the distance toward the land to the Eastward.

CHAPTER 4

"A Fatiguing Scramble"

JULY 28–JULY 31, MACKINAC

WEDNESDAY 28TH [CONTINUED]

The approach to Mackinaw is very fine, the cliffs at the eastern end reminding one a little of the rock of Gibraltar.[1] The town & fort are at the other end of the Island. The town very low & consisting of two streets running parallel with the water. The whole circumference of the island is about 9 miles, & it contains 1200 inhabitants. The village is surrounded by a high cliff, & overlooked by the Fort, which is 150 feet above the lake. More inland about half a mile is an elevation 300 feet above the water, where, upon the spot where stood old Fort Holmes, is an observatory commanding a beautiful & extensive prospect. This is the first highland we have seen since leaving Lockport.

On arriving took the carriage belonging to the Mission House & arrived there in due time.[2] Found it full & got rather inferior

---

1. Mackinac Island at the far north end of Lake Huron, lies near the straits to Lake Michigan. The St. Mary's River, flowing in from Lake Superior, enters Lake Huron forty miles northwest of the island. A trading center since the seventeenth century, Mackinac Island in 1852 was a scenic stopping place on the way to and from other Great Lakes' ports. It had a reputation for pure air, clear water, and magnificent scenery. It was beginning to become a destination resort.
2. Members of a Presbyterian missionary society had taught English, gardening, cooking, and Bible verses to Native American children for fourteen years in a fifty-yard-long three-story building on the hill overlooking Lake Huron. In the 1840s E. A. Franks converted this school building to a hotel and called it the Mission House. According to his advertisement in the *Lake Superior*

accommodation for 2 dollars a day. Our windows looked into a
dirty inclosure [*sic*] belonging to the kitchen, & closed from all
prospect by a steep hill which rose directly beyond. Sat sometime
after on the front piazza looking out upon the beautiful islands
opposite the house & the moon-lit lake sparkling like silver.

Retired a little after 9 O'clock, & being very weary & moreover not having quite recovered from my seasickness, was very glad
to be quietly in bed on "terra firma." Slept soundly, although the
house was in an uproar all night with people coming & going in
two boats from some places on Lake Michigan.

THURSDAY 29TH

Rose & breakfasted late. Wrote a little & went out to see the Fort.[3]
~~The shores of the little island opposite were white with the
wigwams of the Indians, & we could see their canoes near the
shore.~~ A party of them came to the Hotel this morning to sell
berries & among them a squaw with the most masculine & strongly marked face I ever saw. They seem very distrustful & hard to bar-
gain with.[4]

Walked to the Fort & went through it. Met however with no
politeness, & saw none of the officers. It has round it a stockade
fence of timber driven endwise into the ground & pointed at the
top. It did not impress me very favorably, & did not seem at all
impregnable. It occupied more ground than either of the others we
have yet seen. It is entirely commanded by the hill on which stood
Fort Holmes, which seemed to me a great oversight.

Journal, August 5, 1852, in the summer of 1852 Franks extensively remodeled
it for two hundred guests, improved the landscaping and reopened for business. He supplied horses and carriages for guests.

3. Fort Mackinac was built on a high defensible bluff by the British in 1780 after
they abandoned the old French-built Fort Michilimackinac on the Michigan
shore. September 1, 1796, the fort was ceded to the United States, changed
hands again during the War of 1812, and was finally returned to the United
States in 1815.

4. Some Native Americans had stayed in the Mackinac area living in wigwams
and tipis waiting for their government annuities, food, and whiskey. They
sold handmade crafts and local fish and fruit to curious travelers who visited
their villages.

Mrs. Twining was tired & left us for home, we kept on up the hill above mentioned, when after hard & steep climbing we came out upon the mounds of the fortification. Had a splendid view, which amply rewarded our toil, & in trying to find a short cut to the road, lost our way & found ourselves again in front of the Fort.

Took another start & walking I should think about a mile & a half, came to a curious detached rock named the Sugar Loaf. It rises from the midst of the wood & is partially covered with stunted evergreens, a steep path winds round it near the base, & on one side a ladder was placed, & about fifteen feet up we found the entrance to a cave.

There was a level platform at the mouth where we could stand upright, but we were obliged to stoop to enter. Again we could stand up, but the sides & top were very ragged & the edges projected so sharply that we were obliged to move with caution. Here we found a great many names written upon the almost white projections of the rock. It seemed water-worn & the whole rock within & without was full of strange little holes, with the insides nicely polished as by the action of water. I picked up several snail shells near the cave.

We walked back again by the beautiful road shady & cool with a fine breeze, & in attempting to find a shorter cut, again lost ourselves, seeing the old landmark, the Fort. However, by dint of perseverance got home at last in time to dress for dinner.

After dinner wrote, & sat down to mend some stockings. Then came up suddenly a most terrific thunder storm with sharp lightning accompanied by hail, which broke nearly all the windows on one side of the house. Richard brought us two tumblers full of the stones, which were nearly all of the size of Filberts[5] & some as large as walnuts. It was really fearful to hear & see. Mrs. Twining & I went to one of the front windows to see the storm on the lake. It was beautiful; the waves were so high & covered with foam.

Later in the afternoon had another little shower then the sun came out & we had a splendid rainbow a perfect arch resting on the lake. There was another nearly as bright directly over the first. I never saw a more beautiful sight.

This house is called the Mission House because it was built by the Missionary Society, but now the Protestants have left the place

---

5. Hazelnut, about one inch in diameter.

altogether. There is not even a settled minister in the church here, & they depend entirely upon the chaplain of the garrison. All the inhabitants are Roman Catholicks [*sic*] & the only Protestants are the visitors who come from other places.

The table here is very good, & the fish for those who like it, delicious. Here one gets the famous Mackinaw Trout which sometimes weigh 40 pounds. Spent the evening talking with Mrs. Twining & retired between 9 & 10 O'clock.

FRIDAY 30TH

Was late this morning & found almost every body through breakfast when I got down. The air was like a fine November morning in New York, with a fresh breeze which curled the waves nicely.

We all started on a walk to the Arch Rock with Richard as a guide, but after walking some distance found he did not remember the path & were forced upon our own instincts, wandered about ever so long until we came upon a man who was shooting Pigeons. He said he could not direct us so that we could find the direct path, as it was through the thick woods & we were far from the right way, but would go with us, which he did, & after a fatiguing scramble through thickets, & up & down steep places brought us out at the desired spot. He was tall & thin & exceedingly weather worn, & in his appearance with his gun over his shoulder, & his shrewd & quaint conversation, reminded me strongly of Natty Bumpo the scout.[6]

He talked a great deal of Indians & their "natur" & seemed to have a great deal of good sense. He said there was now at the Fort one regiment of 52 men, & that the commanding officer Colonel Williams was a very pleasant & gentlemanly man.[7]

6. James Fenimore Cooper's famous character in the Leatherstocking Tales.
7. Fort Mackinac's commander, thirty-seven-year-old Captain Thomas Williams from Albany, New York, and West Point, was a strict and severe artillery officer who had served in the Mexican-American War. During the Civil War the unpopular Williams was killed at Baton Rouge, Louisiana. His troops reportedly "cheered the rebels for rendering them such a signal service" (typewritten biography, Mackinac State Historic Parks).

The "Arch" we went to see is a great curiosity. Its top is 220 feet above the Lake. It is evidently of volcanic origin. Far below it is a smaller arch through which you can walk on the beach. The view from the top of the Arch (which looked like pictures of the Natural Bridge in Virginia) is very fine, you look toward the north over three or four small islands upon the distant shore of Northern Michigan & far off to the east to Lake Huron. We went home by a very direct path across the cliff. Mrs. Twining was tired out.

When I had a little rested took a walk through the town & visited some of the shops, found everything very dear, & bought nothing but a little bouquet of Indian work.

At the farther end of the town toward the south there seems to be a settlement of Indians. Looking into some of the doors I saw the squaws & some old men making nets, & several pretty young girls doing the household duties, but very few young men. I presume most of the younger ones were half breeds.

Went home & wrote. Dressed & dined. Directly after dinner walked through the town with Mrs. Twining, went as far as the beach extended.

Saw in front of one of the Indian houses a papoos [*sic*] swathed onto a board tightly, arms & all without power of motion, except the head, which nodded & laughed at us in the pleasantest manner possible. It looked fat & quite pretty. A hoop passed over the top of the board projecting in front to prevent injuries (as I supposed) to the head should it fall forward. A little squaw about 12 years old had another fastened upon her back, with the head bobbing about in the back of her neck.

The steamboats today from St. Mary's & Chicago brought an accession of guests to the Mission & the house is filled to overflowing. The company seem to be mostly western people.

SATURDAY 31ST

After breakfast Richard went off shooting, & Mrs. Twining & I took a long walk, as much as 8 miles in all. We went first to the burying ground, which is possessed of no interest. It is new & very few burials have as yet taken place there. We saw but one stone & that was in the military part. The old burying ground is in the village & very small. The graves most of them simply fenced round & without stones or monuments.

From there we walked on through a very highly romantic road for at least three miles, when we came to a large farm with oxen, outbuildings & everything in New England style. We went to the house & asked permission to rest, which was granted very kindly by the woman of the house who handed each of us a large bowl of rich milk cold as ice, which proved very refreshing. She said that she was from Philadelphia & that her husband was a Scotchman. The farm contained 480 acres, & they had 20 cows. As soon as we got into the house, she sat down & began to comb her hair & by the time we left it was fixed in pimplico order, as it was worn 20 years ago. I believe it is the only farm on the Island although there seems to be plenty very rich land in spots all over.

On our way back visited again the site of the old fort, which Mrs. Twining had not seen, & then home pretty well tired. Dined & spent the afternoon reading sewing & talking with Mrs. Twining.

After tea Richard came home. Had gone after dinner in a boat with a young man from Cleveland & "Natty" over on one of the adjacent islands to shoot pigeons. Shot three, which he gave in pay for the gun, & amused himself afterwards shooting at a mark. They called him a very good shot.

Spent the evening in the parlour, where was a party of western ladies & gentlemen. Cannot say I think much of western manners. There is a coarseness & want of refinement about all I have seen yet, & they appear so *new*.

CHAPTER 5

"Wild Looking Places"
AUGUST 1—AUGUST 3, SAULT STE. MARIE

SUNDAY AUGUST 1ST

Directly after breakfast this morning Mrs. Twining & I started to visit the Sugar Loaf rock. It was Novembery like yesterday & the air was clean & sharp. We found it without trouble & from there went to the Arch Rock & home. Poor Mrs. Twining was very tired & could hardly keep on. It sprinkled a little before we got to the house but the sun came out soon afterwards. The walks on this Island are delightful; they are so shady & retired. In all my rambles, & I have been in every part of it, I never out of the village met a single person unless strangers like ourselves.

Wrote. Dined & spent part of the afternoon writing letters. After Tea Mrs. Twining & I took a walk along the cliff looking for the steamer, the *London*, in which we expected to leave this evening.[1] It happened unfortunately to be a slow boat & we were obliged to wait 'till Twelve O'clock before she arrived. As we had expected her every moment all the evening of course we had no sleep, & were besides almost frozen to death. The night was so fearfully cold. I stood on the wharf waiting for the boat to near the land shaking like an aspen.

At last we started & the Captain gave us a very nice stateroom, although it was very dirty & disagreeable to the olfactory nerves. I went after the chambermaid to put clean clothes on the bed, but she said it was not her business, but that a gentleman attended

---

1. The steamer *London* was an old Canadian side-wheeler.

those rooms. She found him, a surly, dirty waiter of about 19 years & he made the beds, & gave us water & we closed our doors at about One O'clock A.M.

MONDAY 2D

I did not undress last night because things looked too dirty & the pillow smelt so that I put my handkerchief between it & my face. Even then had there been the least motion I should have been very sick, but fortunately we had literally a summer sea. Our stateroom had two doors one opening into the dining saloon, the other on the guards.

Arose before 5 O'clock & went on deck. The sun was just risen & everything was covered with a flood of golden light. The clouds all day have been particularly beautiful. The river St. Mary's is 60 miles long, & very interesting, & lovely. It seems to be filled with Islands covered with low trees, & bushes, & green to the water's edge. At the upper end of the river it widens into Lake George which is several miles wide. For some distance the lake is very shallow, not more than three feet deep, even upon the edge of the channel, which is very narrow, & very deep. The water in the channel is dark green & there is a distinct change to a muddy brown.

We stopped twice to unload flour & take in wood, at little wild looking places, with two or three men & a log cabin. Just before reaching Saut [*sic*] Ste Marie we met a steamer from somewhere on the British shore and we kept side by side 'till we arrived at the wharf. The town is 15 miles from Lake Superior.

There are here a great many Indians. You see them everywhere, & from the pure breed through all shades to white. As much as ten miles down the river, two of them hitched their canoe to the steamer & rode in the foam keeping their canoe steady with a paddle & occasionally shouting in the wildest manner.

We met at Mackinaw a Mr. J. Vernon Brown Editor of the *Lake Superior Journal*, a very gentlemanly & intelligent man who resides at Saut Ste Marie & was returning home with his wife. He was very polite on board the boat & advised us to go to the Ste Marie hotel. We did so & he called before dinner to see if we were comfortably located.

This is the oldest town in the United States.[2] It was settled in 1668 by the Jesuits who established here a mission among the Indians. They came from Canada by way of the Lakes. The town contains about 900 inhabitants of whom 100 are Indians.

Fort Brady is here just below the town, surrounded by a high picketted fence at least 20 feet high. They are cedar posts standing endwise as close as possible & sharpened at the top.

Spent the afternoon talking & looking out of the window.

As soon as tea was over a little after half past 6 o'clock we got into a beautiful bark canoe with 2 Indians & went up the rapids or falls of Ste Marie. They are a mile long, & interrupt the navigation between Lake Superior & the lower Lakes. The Indians standing in each end of the canoe first used their paddles or short oars, very quickly & on different sides, then as we got into the foaming & boiling waters they laid them aside & took each a long pole & by long & vigorous pushes, propelled us between the immense boulders which through the clear waters we could see on all sides of us hardly below the surface. The whole fall is about 30 feet.

The scene & its accompaniments was actually splendid. The rushing & foaming of the water, the tossing of our frail bark, the sun setting in gorgeous clouds directly before us, the lonesome melancholy looking shores, & the imperturbability of the Indians who only broke silence occasionally in a few strange sounding gutturals. All made it an undying memory henceforth inerasable.

They drew in to the low tangled looking shore of an Island where one of them steadied the boat in the most wonderful manner, & the other seeing me trying to reach some long hoary looking grey moss, pulled a branch & handed it to me with a sedate smile of satisfaction. The river here as elsewhere is full of Islands & we wound in among them in our perilous course in the most fearful and romantic manner.

We saw a number of canoes with young Indians fishing in the midst of literally speaking the most 'troubled waters.' They were screaming & making all kinds of uncouth noises in apparently great glee. At last we arrived at the upper end in water smooth as glass.

---

2. The French explorer Étienne Brûlé explored Lake Superior in 1621 and Jesuit missionaries reached Sault Ste. Marie, site of a Chippewa village, in 1641. In 1668 Father Jacques Marquette founded a Jesuit Mission there.

At one place where the water was uncommonly fierce the savage before me turned & looked gravely in both our faces, as if to see how much courage we possessed.

The descent was accomplished in four minutes although it had taken us an hour to go up. The principle labour is to keep the boat from upsetting or splitting on the sharp rocks. It cannot be described to give any idea of the reality. I would never advise any one to attempt it who did not possess strong nerves. There was such perfect calmness & self-reliance visible in our Indians that I could not feel the slightest approach to fear.

I sat in the forward part of the canoe & got drenched by the foam & water, which at one time dashed, directly in my face. We saw in our descent in the wildest part, three canoes of wild looking savages dashing up, looking fiercer than the waters themselves. Two of them were women who handled the paddles as dexterously as any of the men.

Soon after our return we had a call from Mr. Brown who was very agreeable. Went to bed about a quarter to Ten.

TUESDAY 3D

Arose after a refreshing sleep in a clean & comfortable bed, the most to my taste since leaving home. Breakfasted, & arranged my trunk a little. Just before ten Mr. Brown called & brought with him several fine sketches of the town & neighborhood done by a Mr. Metcalf,[3] an artist who spent some months in this region painting & sketching.

We then went to the Fort,[4] where the Governor of Michigan Mr. McClellan[5] reviewed the troops in company with a Canadian

---

3. Perhaps Pennsylvania artist John Metcalf or painter W. F. Metcalf.
4. In 1822, U.S. soldiers built Fort Brady as a border post to counter the British garrison at Drummond Island. Fort Brady was briefly abandoned in 1848 after the Mexican War but in 1849 was reoccupied in response to threatened Native American hostilities.
5. Forty-five-year-old Robert McClelland, originally from Pennsylvania, was elected governor of Michigan on November 4, 1851, and in 1852 re-elected for two more years. In sparsely populated Marquette County he had received a landslide fifty-three votes. McClelland had been a member of Congress from 1843 to 1845 and 1847 to 1849, where he had supported antislavery

officer. The commander of the Fort is Captain Getty[6] with two lef-tenants [*sic*]. The buildings inside the Fort surrounded a beautiful green square where they went through their evolutions, commenc-ing by giving the governor a salute of 15 guns. He is a very plain farmer looking man & wore spectacles.

After the review, walked through a part of the Indian quarter & looked into several of the wigwams. They were most of them built of bark with but one apartment, where were in some instances beds in the separate corners, & people setting upon the floor. All of them here are of the Chippiwa [*sic*] tribe & they are poor & miser-able. Most of them, particularly the young ones seemed to have considerable white blood in their veins. Some of the young squaws are very pretty.

On our way home bought some miserable cakes & soda bis-cuit & on our return to our quarters, lunched upon these & a glass of iced water. Wrote, dined. Took a nap & read 'till tea time. Spent the evening looking out of the window, without a light & went to bed about nine. In the course of the afternoon had a little shower.

measures. He soon became secretary of the interior serving Franklin Pierce who was elected U.S. president later in 1852.

6. Thirty-three-year-old Captain George Washington Getty, an 1840 West Point graduate who had fought under General Winfield Scott in Mexico.

CHAPTER 6

"Boundary of Civilization"
AUGUST 4–AUGUST 15, LAKE SUPERIOR

Wednesday 4th

Started in the Steamer *Baltimore*[1] for Eagle Harbour a little after Ten. Before leaving the Hotel had a conversation with a Mr. Backus who belonged to the land office & who shewed us some maps of the mining tour, & ships on the Lake. He very politely gave us all the information in his power.[2]

We rode a mile over the portage on the flat freight car which carried our baggage. The trunks answered very well for seats. All the merchandise, & the supplies for the Lake settlements are carried

---

1. Built in 1847 in Monroe, Michigan, on Lake Erie, the wooden *Baltimore* was a 169-foot-long, 26-foot-wide side-wheel freight and passenger steamboat. Earlier in 1852, men, horses, and oxen had hauled this 513-ton steamboat on rollers a few feet a day for a mile overland and around the St. Mary's rapids to Lake Superior. The *Baltimore*, four other small steamships, and dozens of sailing schooners on Lake Superior supplied the miners and settlers. On June 18, 1855, the *Baltimore* returned to Lake Huron, becoming the second vessel to pass through the new Soo Canal. Later in 1855 the *Baltimore* parted her anchor cable in a storm and crashed ashore at Sheboygan, Wisconsin. She became a total loss.
2. In 1846, *A True Description of the Lake Superior Country* for pleasure travelers described the romance of outdoor camping and paddling a voyageur canoe. By 1852, concentrated copper in the uplifted rocks along Keweenaw Peninsula's fifty-mile geological fault line was beginning to be exploited; a number of mines had opened, financed mainly by investors in New England and New York. Eagle Harbor and Eagle River provided landing places for ships to unload supplies and load up copper ore.

over this little railway.[3] There were not many passengers, only four ladies.

There was an Indian on board who was being carried to Marquette the county town, to be tried for murder. His poor mother was with him, & looked sad enough.

The Governor & a judge were on board. The judge's name was Goodwin;[4] & we picked an acquaintance with him, finding him a very agreeable pleasant man.

We passed several small Islands during the day, or rather points of rock covered with trees. The north shore near which we passed was bold & in some places highly picturesque. Toward night the weather changed from bright to gloomy, & there was a very thick fogg. I spent all the afternoon in the saloon reading & talking with the judge. In the evening we were regaled with music for an hour by four or five performers on the violin Clarionet [sic] Horn etc.

The Captain was not on board owing to illness, & the owner, A Mr. McNight of Saut Ste Marie[5] took his place. Mr. Backus had introduced us to him before starting & we found him very polite & attentive. In the evening he shewed us a chart drawn by an English Officer of the Lake, & pointed out different points of interest. Went to bed at half past Ten O'clock.

---

3. The rapids of the St. Mary's River prevented all vessels but canoes from going between Lakes Superior and Huron. A small railroad track had been built for the portage around the rapids. The Soo Canal, allowing navigable water traffic between the two lakes, did not open until 1855.

4. Fifty-three-year-old Judge Daniel Goodwin. He had been recently elected the first district judge for the newly formed Upper Peninsula Judicial District. A New York native, Judge Goodwin had presided over the first Michigan State constitutional convention in 1837. He had been United States district attorney for the District of Michigan under the Jackson and Van Buren administrations and judge of the Michigan Supreme Court and of the Detroit Circuit from 1843 to 1846.

5. Forty-two-year-old Sheldon McKnight owned several vessels and was instrumental in building the small railroad around the St. Mary's River rapids. He had been appointed by President Polk in 1845 to study the mineral resources of the Upper Peninsula.

THURSDAY 5TH

Awoke & found we were lying in the harbour of Marquette, or Carp River. Here our judge & the prisoner left us.[6]

It is a beautiful spot in a cove of the Lake with forest & high ground surrounding it on all sides & rising directly from the water. It was very early hardly Five O'clock & damp & raw in the extreme. There is a mountain a few miles back with rich Iron mines, & extensive Iron works on the bank.[7] Several pretty houses were just finished & in course of erection, & I thought, that if it was not quite so far from the rest of the world I might be content to spend a part of my life here. Did not go on shore. The wharf & passage way were so littered with freight discharging from the boat.

After leaving this place we passed for some miles close to the northern shore. There is a high mountain range just inland which reminded me strongly of the distant Catskills.[8] One of the summits was a facsimile of Saddleback near Williamstown.[9] Near it was a high pyramidal rock which rose evenly against the sky.

Lake Superior is 420 miles long & 135 wide, in some places 900 feet deep. The shores are generally high & its waters peculiarly clear. In one place we lost sight of land on both sides but generally sail close to the southern shore.

Sat on deck all the morning. After dinner passed Manitou Island which is about 2 miles long north & south. It is just opposite Kaiwaina Point.[10] After this the boat followed the southern shore closely 'till we arrived at Copper harbour.

The shore is everywhere the same low at the water & rising directly behind to sometimes the height of 300 feet. Copper harbour is nearly hidden from view in a cove which is entered on one

---

6. The day he left the *Baltimore*, August 5, Judge Goodwin held his first court in Marquette County in a small office building adjoining the Northwestern Hotel. There Judge Goodwin presided over the Indian's murder indictment and other indictments for forgery and larceny.

7. One month earlier, on July 7, Marquette Iron Company had shipped the first barrels of iron ore to leave the Upper Peninsula.

8. A mountain range just west of the Hudson River between New York City and Albany.

9. Williamstown, in western Massachusetts.

10. Keweenaw Point, the tip of Keweenaw Peninsula.

side where on the eastern point is a lighthouse, & just before the entrance is a fort on the border of a little lake 2 miles long nearly hidden by the foliage. There were no more than a dozen houses in the place, which lay at the foot of a steep spur of the coast range of highlands.[11] We went on shore & picked up some pebbles on the beach. The boat staid two hours loading & unloading.

As soon as we started had tea, & at about 8 stopped at Eagle Harbour. Here again we entered a deep cove, round which the town is built. The banks were precipitous blocks of red sandstone mostly & the town was imbedded in dry shifting sand in which the foot sinks to the ankle at every step. There are two Hotels & a public square & it looks prettily from the harbour. The mines are several miles back in the mountain. We were detained here more than two hours & did not arrive at Eagle River 'till half past 12 O'clock.

For some time before landing we had a brilliant display of the Aurora Borealis. It appeared in the form of an arch of brilliant white light the two ends resting on the lake & in which it was reflected like the moon. In the center of the black space under the arch shone the north star. We could scarcely believe that day was not dawning above the black wall that seemed close to us. It was intensely cold.

We landed on a scow[12] which we had towed from Eagle Harbour as the Lake was too shallow to allow the steamer to go to the wharf.

Mr. McKnight introduced us on board to a Judge Campbell[13]

---

11. According to the 1850 census only 185 pioneering families lived on the entire Keweenaw Peninsula. Hardworking, hard-drinking bachelor Cornish, Irish, and German miners lived in log cabins and a few frame houses near the mines. A few managers brought families. For the most part, tree stumps, roaming pigs, ducks, chickens, and dogs, and all manner of out buildings like privies, sheds, and coops characterized the tiny settlements. A few merchants had opened stores.

12. A square-ended, flat-bottomed boat, here used primarily to carry ore.

13. James Valentine Campbell, a twenty-nine-year-old lawyer from Detroit, originally from New York, who had traveled to the Upper Peninsula several times. From 1858 to 1890 he became justice of the Michigan Supreme Court and a professor of law at the University of Michigan. Mining company lawyers and a few private practitioners occasionally traveled to the Keewenaw Peninsula to handle what little legal business there was. No lawyers resided permanently in the Upper Peninsula.

who resides here, & he turned out to be quite a character. He was very polite & before leaving the steamer took us into the Steward's pantry where we got a cup of coffee without milk, & a biscuit & butter.

We landed on a long planked wharf & walked through the deepest, dryest [*sic*] sand I ever saw to the Hotel kept by Mr. Chamberlin.[14] They were all asleep, & the judge routed out the Landlord & his wife to give up their bed to us. Almost all our passengers landed, the Governor among them, to whom I was introduced by Judge Campbell. Richard slept on a couch in the parlour. Although our bed did not look or smell the cleanest, I slept soundly till half past six in the morning of—

FRIDAY 6TH

Breakfasted, and as the Governor & all the gentlemen were going to visit the mines, we deferred our visit 'till tomorrow. Spent the morning on the beach west of the town looking for Agates. We were not very successful getting but a few very small ones. An Indian came & sitting down by us began searching & after finding a few offered to sell them to us. There was a funny little Indian child about two years old who ran about the beach & seemed quite sociable.

Dined, during dinner had a pleasant conversation with the Governor who sat opposite to me & was very sociable. Took a little walk in the woods & brought home some leaves to press. Wrote & talked with the Judge. Took a walk with him to the falls of Eagle River & got home just in time for tea. After tea ~~almost~~ all the passengers who had landed with us left in the return boat. We went down on the beach with the Judge to see the boat off.

Spent the evening talking with him in the parlour & retired at about Ten O'clock. To-night we took possession of a nice room

---

14. Enterprising families opened their homes to travelers. Early hotels were small. H. B. Chamberlain, age thirty, originally from New York, had "greatly enlarged and newly furnished" his log Eagle River House, "pleasantly located near the lake." He advertised that, "horses and carriages will be furnished to those wishing to visit the mines" (Eagle River Hotel advertisement, *Lake Superior Journal*, August 5, 1852).

with two beds, looking off on the Lake, which Richard & I occupy,
Mrs. Twining preferring one by herself.

SATURDAY 7TH

After breakfast Mrs. Twining & I went with the Judge to visit the
Phenix [*sic*] mine a mile back from the Lake. We had a pleasant
walk through a clearing, the tall black stumps standing in all direc-
tions in the midst of oats & potatoes.

We arrived at the Office of the Superintendent, in a slight
sprinkling, which however did not last long. We went first to the
place where the ore is broken up after being brought up in buckets
from the shaft. From thence to the room where these smaller
pieces are ground by heavy stamps to a coarse powder. Then we
watched it through the washing process, & looked down the deep
shaft 150 feet. It is worked by a small steam engine.[15]

We were very politely treated, & accompanied home by a Mr.
Chipman,[16] a young lawyer of Detroit, who in a fit of despair on
being refused by the parents of a lady to whom he was very much
attached married a full blooded squaw. She is not here with him &
he boards in the house with us. He is pleasant & gentlemanly &
quite young.

In the afternoon, we all went in a waggon with two horses to
visit the Cliff Mine,[17] three miles back from the landing. The road

---

15. The underground copper was broken into manageable pieces by hand,
    hauled up the mineshafts by horse-powered whims winding up a cable. After
    grinding, the ore was loaded into barrels and then hauled to the docks in
    horse-drawn wagons. At peak times up to one hundred tons a month came to
    the Lake Superior shores. There the copper was loaded on schooners, carried
    across the St. Mary's rapids, and reshipped to eastern smelters.
16. J. Logan Chipman, a twenty-two-year-old prospective lawyer from Detroit.
    He had been an explorer for the Montreal Mining Company and participated
    in making the treaty of Detroit with Ottawa and Chippewa tribes. He was
    admitted to the bar in 1854 and later became a politician, Detroit city attor-
    ney, Superior Court judge, and U.S. congressman.
17. In 1846 masses of pure copper had been found in a cliff face inland from
    Eagle River. Pure copper boulders weighing up to fifty tons were buried in
    the cliff. In 1852, the Cliff Mine was the largest, most productive, and most
    profitable copper mine on the peninsula.

was dreadfully rough ascending the coast range & descending again on the other side, through a thick forest with a few trees cut down occasionally on the sides of the road. The wife of one of the superintendents rode up with us with her baby.

There is quite a village around the works, & in the little graveyard they were digging a grave as we passed. I believe accidents are not unusual. The miners are many of them Cornish men used to mining in England.

We went first to the office, where we saw some very beautiful specimens & from there all around as at the Phenix. The works at all the mines are the same only some are much more extensive, with more powerful machinery. The engine of the Cliff Mine is immense & very powerful. The deepest shaft is 520 feet deep, with many passages, running north & south at different levels. The value of the copper taken out last year was 280,000 dollars.

There is a Methodist missionary here & a small building appropriated for a church & school house.[18]

We walked a short distance to the North American which was the same although much smaller. We were everywhere treated with great politeness & attention. From all I saw & heard, I should think that intemperance was the crying evil.

We rode home down hill in much quicker time than we went, & were jolted nearly to death over the uneven road. Took tea & spent the evening conversing with the Judge & Mr. Chipman. Retired at Ten.

SUNDAY 8TH

Breakfasted & spent the morning in my room writing.

There is no church here, & there seems to be no sabbath. Perhaps there is not quite so much carting of copper & barrels; but the stores are open, & seem to do a better business than in the week days for the miners can then have leisure to furnish themselves with what they need, as they cease labour early Saturday afternoon.

18. Reverend John Pitizel had formed a small congregation of Cornish miners and established the Cliff Mine Church. During the summer 1852 he held a Methodist camp meeting for hundreds of Chippewa, who adopted him into the tribe and named him "Yellow Beard."

Rode on horseback with the Judge & got home to a late tea. We followed a trail through a dense forest where the tall trees met above, & constant care was necessary to keep from being torn by the thick underbrush. It was perfectly delightful, because so entirely new to me. The road, if road it could be called, was in some places excessively rough & bad, & I let my horse pick his own way, which he did very carefully. We dismounted near a deserted wigwam, & rested ourselves. I never enjoyed any thing more in my life.

Spent the evening with the two gentlemen & retired about Ten.

MONDAY 9TH

After a restless night not having slept more than four hours, arose & breakfasted. Walked with Mrs. Twining & the Judge on the beach.

Left there & climbed the high bank at its termination, & pursuing a narrow steep trail for a long distance along the rocky shore, had a delightful walk. When I was tired I sat down on a fallen tree, leaning my head against another & quietly enjoyed the beauty of the scene. I looked off at the beautiful lake & the dim shore of Isle Royale in the distant north west, & tried to realize that I was indeed on the Lake Superior that my map pictured on the northern boundary of civilization, & I am not certain even then that I did fully. I remained however entransed [sic] & delighted I know not how long, soothed by the rushing sound of the waves against the rock & delivering myself to all kinds of strange fancies.

When I returned I met Richard who was gun in hand enjoying himself to his hearts content. Dined in the afternoon. Took a long walk with the Judge, through the thickest, tallest forest I ever saw or expect to see. We came out on the beach at Sand bay, & sat down a few moments.

After our return home, we all went out in a row boat, Richard & the Judge rowing. We passed round the propeller *Independence*[19] which lay out in the Lake taking in copper from a flat boat. Until the water was over a hundred feet deep, could see the bottom distinctly. Had a pleasant time, & after tea finished with a game of whist.

---

19. A 280-ton vessel owned by Captain Bristol & Co.

TUESDAY 10TH

Was disturbed at half past four by a man knocking up Richard to go shooting pigeons, & did not sleep much afterward. Breakfasted, & spent the whole morning in the parlour arguing with the Judge & Mr. Chipman. Dined, & walked on the piazza with the Judge. Mr. Chipman gave me a ride in a baby's waggon. Wrote. Took a walk up the Lake in the woods with the Judge & sat a while to rest. The Mosquitos & little biting sand flies are the plague of all the woods in this part of the country. I was bitten dreadfully & looked as though covered with blotches. Spent most of the evening lying on my bed as I was both sleepy & tired.

WEDNESDAY 11TH

Breakfasted & read law, talking occasionally with the gentlemen. After dinner packed up, & went on board a sail boat belonging to a merchant here, Mr. Senter.[20]

The Judge went with us, & a Dr. Clark.[21] Mr. Chipman went on board with us to bid us good bye. The wind was quite variable, sometimes sufficiently fresh to make Mrs. T & I feel rather uncomfortably. We passed Sand bay & Cat harbour, & some boulders of dark conglomerate & arrived in 2 hours at Eagle Harbour, & went to the Atwood house.[22]

---

20. John Senter, age twenty-eight, from New Hampshire, was Eagle River's postmaster and an agent for blasting powder and insurance. He owned a general store at Eagle River and sold necessities such as preserved meats, flour, sugar, spices, kitchenware, men's clothes, fabrics (for women's clothes), and tools. He also did a good business in liquor and wine.

21. Dr. Luther W. Clarke, twenty-seven years old, from Ohio. He settled in Michigan in 1847 and lived in Eagle River.

22. The Atwood House's *Lake Superior Journal* advertisement of May, 1852, read: "This Hotel, pleasantly situated on the West side of the Harbor, was opened last year by the Present Proprietors and has been enlarged and newly fitted up for the accommodation of visitors to this interesting portion of the mineral country." The Hotel furnished "conveyances to those wishing to visit the mines."

An express locomotive, its large driving wheels capable of forty-mile-an-hour speeds, pulls into the market at Syracuse, New York. (*Ballou's Pictorial*, August 1856)

The multiple cascades of Trenton Falls in New York State and the rich fossils found in its picturesque chasm attract eastern tourists. (*Gleason's Pictorial*, December 1852)

Niagara Falls visitors view the American Falls and the Niagara Gorge from the shore near Hog's Back and Terrapin Tower, one of several observation towers. (*Gleason's Pictorial*, July 1852)

According to legend, giant fairies that once inhabited Mackinac Island formed the Arch Rock by flying nearly 150 feet above the lake and more than 50 feet across. (*Harper's New Monthly Magazine*, March 1853

In Sault Ste. Marie a small railroad portage around the St. Mary's River rapids carries travelers and goods between Lake Huron and Lake Superior. (*Harper's New Monthly Magazine*, March 1853)

Fort Mackinac's cedar stockade and blockhouses dominate the view of Mackinac village and Indian tepees on the beach. (*Gleason's Pictorial*, May 1855)

The northwoods meet the Lake Superior shore at Eagle Harbor, which displays the untamed beauty of Michigan's Upper Peninsula. (*Harper's New Monthly Magazine*, April 1853)

Immense engines, stamping mills, and conveyers of the prosperous Cliff Mine process ore from the Keewenaw copper cliffs. (*Harper's New Monthly Magazine*, March 1853)

The remote commercial village of Copper Harbor on Lake Superior initiated travelers to the sparsely settled Michigan copper country. (*Harper's New Monthly Magazine*, March 1853)

From Galena, Illinois, wedged between rocky, lead-filled hills, steam boats navigate the narrow Fever River to the Mississippi. (*Harper's New Monthly Magazine*, July 1853)

In grief over lost love, an Indian princess leapt off Maiden's Rock on Lake Pepin in the upper Mississippi River, one of many American cliffs inspiring similar legends. (*Harper's New Monthly Magazine*, July 1853

St. Paul, capital of the Minnesota Territory, attracted settlers with abundant waterpower, established trading posts, and ready river transportation. (*Harper's New Monthly Magazine*, July 1853)

The Falls of St. Anthony halted navigation on the Mississippi and at the same time lured travelers to visit the upper river and its environs. (*Harper's New Monthly Magazine*, July 1853)

Little Crow Village on the Mississippi was named for a tribal leader who had sought peace when Sioux ceded Minnesota to the United States in return for money and provisions. (*Gleason's Pictorial*, July 1854)

Imposing stone Fort Snelling, a supply depot a the junction of the Mississippi and St. Peter's rivers, built to defend against Indians and English, never saw battle. (*Ballou's Pictorial*, August 1855)

The laughing waters of Little Falls were renamed Minnehaha Falls in 1852 and were later made famous in Longfellow's *Song of Hiawatha*. (*Harper's New Monthly Magazine*, July 1853)

The lead region around Galena, Illinois, and Dubuque, Iowa, supported settlement and vital commerce on the upper Mississippi. (*Harper's New Monthly Magazine*, July 1853)

Barrels, bales, bags, and boxes at the St. Louis levee are destined for the Mississippi and its tributaries on dozens of steamboats docking daily. (*Ballou's Pictorial*, March 1857)

Steamboat traffic crowds the public landing at the principal Ohio River port, Cincinnati, a wealthy commercial metropolis founded in 1788. (*Gleason's Pictorial*, April 1855)

Trains on the financially troubled Erie Railroad soar 110 feet over the Starrucca Creek Valley, Pennsylvania, on the stone viaduct, an engineering marvel. (*Harper's New Monthly Magazine*, July 1850)

It was one of the first built upon the shore of the Lake & is of logs, filled between with mortar neither papered or seiled [*sic*], & it looked oddly to see pictures hung against the bare logs & the wall above formed of boards resting on large beams or in other words the lower side of the floor above. They had been to tea but got up a very nice one for us. Went immediately to bed. The partitions were every where so thin that we could hear every thing said or done in the house.

THURSDAY 12TH

Arose to a late breakfast, & immediately afterward went to the Copper Falls mine.

We stopped & alighted at the house of a Mr. Hill[23] whose wife received us very pleasantly, being introduced by the Judge.

The house although of logs & very rude in construction still had an air of refinement, with its couch, centre table of books & guitar in the corner of its little parlor. We took off our bonnets & shawls, & were provided by Mrs. Hill with sacks to prevent our soiling our dresses, & a pair of India Rubbers for me. I tied my handkerchief over my head & we descended the hill a short distance to where we could enter by a horizontal passage with a railway & car for bringing out the ore.

We were joined here by Mr. Hill & Doctor Hanchett a very fine looking man who was dressed for the purpose very appropriately in dark pants & red flannel shirt very open & turned back at the throat. The Judge, Richard & Mr. Hill looked like frights, each being provided with a coat & hat impossible to describe for quaintness & age.

After walking along awhile cautiously in a low wet muddy

---

23. The 1850 census lists a James Hill, thirty-six, a miner, and his wife, Jane, thirty, both born in England, as residents of Lower Houghton County where the Copper Falls mine is located. A Samuel Worth Hill, a Vermont native thirty-six years old, was a respected pioneer miner, surveyor, and local character who had been among the first to make valuable copper discoveries in the region. According to legend his reputation for cursing inspired the expression, "What the Sam Hill?" Sam is not listed in the 1850 census of Houghton County.

place by the light of pieces of candle carried by the gentlemen, we were met by a miner with the intimation that there would be a blast directly & must remain out of danger. We all stopped & before long a number of miners came along passing us 'till the explosion was over. It came with a strangely unpleasant sensation through the cave & a dull heavy sound & we heard the pieces of rock falling in some paralel [*sic*] passage above us, presently the smoke rushed past & around us & a strong smell of gunpowder. Soon after we were told four other blasts were lighted. After waiting about 20 minutes the explosions followed each other rapidly & we proceeded on our way.

We saw the whole process & the miners at their work, & went out as we came into the warm light of day. The passages of course were cold & damp.

On our way to the mine we saw a young woman with guitar sitting in a window, & were told it was common. On our return to Mr. Hill's we were offered wine & they gave us some beautiful specimens. Had a very hot drive home 5 miles.

Dined, read & wrote. We saw running about tame near the house a young Gull. They are dark grey while young but turn white as they grow older. Took a walk with the Judge to the Indian quarter & looked into several wigwams. The sand was so unpleasantly deep that I was glad to get home again.

After tea we all went to the beach & sat on a platform of boards in front of a stove on some chairs 'till 9 O'clock when we went home & retired.

FRIDAY 13TH

As soon as breakfast was over walked to the beach to see a very large Trout just caught. It was beautiful looking & weighed 36 pounds.

Spent the morning in the parlour reading & talking to the Judge. The woman of the house is very talkative & meddlesome & I kept as much out of her way as possible. Made a most miserable dinner & afterwards walked to the lighthouse. Went up into the lantern where everything was neat as possible, spoke to two or three Indians who were engaged making nets & smoking in their wigwams. One was a fur trader & quite intelligent.

About four O'clock the *Baltimore* came in & we went on board for Ontonagon leaving Richard to join us on our return. The propeller *Manhattan* started just after us & we raced all night. It was very rough all night & we had high wind with very vivid lightning towards morning.

[SATURDAY — 14TH]

Very early in the morning we cast anchor off the Ontonagon river, about a quarter of a mile. It was so very rough that it was not considered advisable for the ladies to try to get ashore, but after breakfast we got into a bateau[24] or freight boat with Mr. and Mrs. Backus & visited the town.[25]

It looks very pleasantly from the river with its trees & white buildings, but on landing you find yourself as deep in the sand as at all the other places on this lake. It is situated on the Ontonagon River, which is navigable for small steamboats about 30 miles to the rapids. The mines here are from eighteen to twenty miles back in the mountain.

A Mr. Beaser[26] took us to see his garden, which was very flourishing, containing a great many kinds of vegetables & flowers, & he showed us also a very nice hen house built tight & warm for the winter. We also made another call & went back to the wharf where the gentlemen brought chairs & we sat 'till the boat was ready for us to leave again.

We saw a number of Indians, three of whom were the wildest I ever saw. Two of them were wrapped in blankets, & one had the tail of a squirrel wound round his head. One of them helped row the bateau & was dressed in such a manner, that every movement he showed his brawny bare legs to the thigh.

We had four oxen on board who were sent on shore in the water with their heads held up each side of a little boat, two at a time. It was very hard for the poor creatures & they looked perfectly exhausted when they landed. A horse on board was sent ashore

---

24. A long, light, flat-bottomed boat with a sharply pointed bow and stern, used especially in Canada and the northeast United States.
25. In 1851, Ontonagon had seven log houses; by 1852, 103 frame buildings composed the town, then the largest on the Lake Superior shore.
26. Martin Beaser, twenty-nine, a merchant originally from New York. He valued his property at four thousand dollars in 1850.

in the bateau. At Eleven we started again down the lake.

We had been about 400 miles from Ste Marie, & has [*sic*] seen as much as was possible. On shore beyond Ontonagon rose the Porcupine mountain, looking high & blue in the distance, & the dark green water around us in high foaming waves. It was difficult to keep up through the day it was so rough.

Just as tea was ready we arrived off Eagle River & the Judge left us. I went to bed very early, hearing the last thing the sound of the music, to which the gentlemen were dancing. They had no ladies for partners.

I should have mentioned that when we arrived at Eagle Harbour Richard joined us again, & Dr. Clark, Mr. Chipman & Judge Goodwin visited us, the latter staying some time.

Sunday 15th

Did not get up 'till 10 O'clock when we were lying at the wharf of Marquette. The country around & the little Islands looked beautifully, & just behind us I noticed again Saddleback & the Pyramid mountain I mentioned before. Did not go ashore. At half past Ten had service in the saloon & a sermon by a Methodist missionary, was not particularly interested, & as soon as it was finished went directly to my room sick enough. Suffered constantly through the day from sea-sickness.

About 3 O'clock stopped at Grand Island & we all went on shore for a ramble. There was an immense quantity of Whortleberries[27] which we picked and ate. Went to the house of the only inhabitant, a Mr. Williams[28] who owns nearly all the Island. Saw his wife & in a bed in the room we were in was a boy

---

27. Sweet black berries on a low spreading shrub, related to the common blueberry, also known as bog bilberry.

28. Originally from Vermont, Abraham Williams was the first white settler on the south central shore of Lake Superior. His friend Chief Omenominee had invited him to live on Grand Island and the Williams family moved there July 30, 1840. Williams and his wife built several log cabins and raised twelve children on the island. He helped later settlers build cabins on the peninsula shore. Williams' trading post on Grand Island was a regular stop for vessels on Lake Superior.

of 13 years, who had had fits from the time he was three months old, & was a dreadful image of pain & suffering. He had lost both eyes & looked like a corpse. It is said that Mr. Williams does not like to have his children settle on the Island but sends them off as soon as they marry.

This Island is about nine miles long in the form of a crescent, & very beautiful. In one part the coast was rocky & fantastic in the extreme. We sailed between it & the south shore of the Lake & it seemed as though we were in a beautiful winding river. The picture rocks commence before well leaving Grand Island. They are of Limestone & 300 feet high. The commencement was a log cabin, next a tower or shrine of the virgin, then came a long row of bat-tlemented walls & towers, next the chapel & parsonage, which were very beautiful, next a city with every variety of building & decoration.

As we passed on there was a sloop in full sail & some tents pitched close to the water, then came the famous arch with its lit-tle side arch that a boat can sail through, then again the bastions & walls. One can imagine any thing almost, in the variegated rock, the different colours being caused by the water dripping through the uneven face of the rock. It is all crowned with a thick forest, which looks like beautiful gardens in the background.

We were all very much obliged to the captain, or Mr. Whiting who acted in the absence of the captain who went out of his way 95 miles to give us a fine view of all the wonders of the Lake. Soon after tea he called me to see the Grand Sable a sandbank 300 feet high, of white sea sand about two miles long. It reminded me of the coast of the desert of Sahara. Retired about Ten.

Richard was quite sick with Diaroeha [*sic*] chills & fever.

CHAPTER 7

"Very Rough"

AUGUST 16–AUGUST 22, LAKE MICHIGAN, MACKINAC, AND CHICAGO

MONDAY 16TH

Was awakened by the boat [*Baltimore*] stopping & thought we had arrived at our destination. Found however we were only landing in Whiskey bay. It was very foggy & we were detained by it some time, finally came to the wharf at the Saut Ste Marie, have been absent on our trip up the Lake 12 days. Sat on our baggage on the car to the Ste Marie Hotel where we arrived at 10 O'clock.

Wrote. Dined & went to the post office with Richard. Read 'till tea time.

Immediately after tea went on board the steamer *London* bound for Mackinaw. Mr. & Mrs. Backus came on board to bid us good bye. Mr. Senter was also on board on his way to New York.

The river St Marie looked beautifully. We sat on deck watching the changing banks, with their Indian wigwams & groups, & the picturesque Islands 'till dusk when we drew up to a small wharf near two Indian wigwams on the Canada shore & made fast for the night. On account of hidden rocks & Islands it is not considered safe to run with boats at night. Richard & I went on shore for a walk. It was a pretty spot with wild flowers & tall trees. We picked a pretty bunch of flowers & spent the rest of the evening in the saloon talking.

The boat was crowded & the captain's clerk gave up his nice large room to us. It was the best on board with a double french bedstead nicely curtained. Slept nicely & awoke about 3 O'clock as we were starting again. Took another nap however & rose in time for breakfast.

TUESDAY 17TH

We did not arrive at Mackinaw 'till about 12 O'clock. A miner had some beautiful specimens of copper on board which he was showing the passengers. Mrs. Twining & I bought a few. Sat in the saloon reading all the morning. On getting to Mackinaw went to the Mission House & got three nice rooms. Dined, read & mended all the afternoon. After tea Mrs. Twining & I took a walk past the spring to the beach.

Richard was not well, & retired early.[1]

WEDNESDAY 18TH

Breakfasted & sent to the Fort for Dr. Bailey.[2] He soon came & prescribed for Richard who spent the morning lying on my bed. I sat beside him most of the time sewing. Wrote. Dined. Read all the afternoon. After tea sat on the piazza talking with Mrs. Twining 'till half past eight, when the Doctor came to my room & sat with me 'till 10 - 1/2. Found him very pleasant & full of anecdote & information. He invited us to go sailing the next day.

THURSDAY 19TH

Soon after breakfast came the Doctor to say the boat was ready if we were & soon after we started for the beach with a Mrs. Clark of Detroit. The boat was rowed by six soldiers from the Fort, & we went entirely round the Island, stopping near an hour on the beach

---

1. Mackinac Island's pure air and refreshing climate had given it a reputation as a healthy spot. "An ague [fever], contracted below, has been known to cease even before the patient has set his foot on the island," wrote a Cincinnati physician in 1842. "Bowel complaints seldom prevail," said the 1870 Fort Mackinac surgeon, Dr. H. R. Mills (Eugene P. Peterson, *Mackinac Island: Its History in Pictures*, 1973, 27, 49).

2. Captain Joseph Howard Bailey, a thirty-eight-year-old doctor from New York, had been appointed directly into the army at age twenty and served as assistant surgeon at Fort Mackinac from 1852 to 1856. In 1853, his daughter Mary married Captain Williams, the commander of Fort Mackinac. After Captain Bailey retired from the Army in 1862 he lived on Mackinac Island.

at the British ferry. We saw in succession the arch rock, the lovers leap, the chimney rock, & Robinson's folly, of which last the story is, that having run away with a beautiful Indian girl he refused to give her up & being pursued by her friends, jumped with her from this high cliff into the lake.

The day was clear & beautiful & we enjoyed it exceedingly. Got home just in time for dinner. Dr. Bailey dined with us. He is a great favorite with everybody. Wrote a letter & laid [*sic*] down. Spent the evening in the parlour talking with Mrs. Twining. Went to bed about 9 O'clock.

Had hardly composed myself comfortably before Mr. Frank the landlord knocked at the door, saying that the Propeller for Chicago was coming.[3] Got up & dressed in the greatest hurry possible & went on board at half past 10. The wind was blowing very fresh, but lulled as we left the land & we had a very comfortable night.

FRIDAY 20TH

Stopped at the North Manitou Island early in the morning to take in wood, & did not leave 'till half past eight. Richard & I took a walk in the woods, which cover the whole Island & are very thick & high. A Mr. Rose also went on shore & walked with us. He seemed well acquainted around Salem, Lynn & Marblehead. Was a fellow passenger from Eagle Harbour down. The Manitou Islands must be some miles in extent, for it was two hours before we passed them all, I believe two or three. At half past Ten we passed Sleeping Bear Point an immense sand bank, so called from a supposed resemblance in a clump of trees on the summit, over 300 feet high. It was so thick & we so far off, 8 miles, that we did not discern the likeness. From this time 'till night we were in the open lake without a vestige of land on any side. We amused ourselves as we could on deck & reading & retired at 9. In the afternoon passed the Propeller *St. Joseph* bound up.

---

3. The wooden *Buffalo* was a one-year-old 650-ton propeller-driven passenger and freight steamboat. Propeller-driven steamboats were relatively new on the lakes and more economical to operate than the side-wheel steamers.

SATURDAY 21

Found on rising that we were lying at the long wharf of Milwaukie [*sic*] & after breakfast the steward ordered a carriage for us & we rode about the city for two hours.

It is situated on both sides of the river Milwaukie, which is navigable for sloops three or four miles beyond. It contains over 23,000 inhabitants & is well built, mostly of yellow brick, which gives it a light pretty appearance. The country rises on each side of the river & some of the finest residences are on the heights. Stopped at a few of the dry goods stores & found them well furnished. They complain that trade is leaving them, since the completion of some of the lower rail-roads.

We did not leave till half past one. It was very rough, & I could scarcely manage to eat my dinner. About an hour after leaving Milwaukie we stopt [*sic*] at Racine.

I did not go on shore as we staid so short a time. All these Lake ports are obliged to build long piers for steamers as the water shoals near the shore & it makes it unpleasant landing. This town has 3000 inhabitants & looked very pretty from the boat & is most of it high like Milwaukie, & built of the same yellow brick.

We passed Kenosha so far off that we could only see that it was a collection of houses, nothing further. Here I became so very sick, that I took to my berth & did not again make my appearance 'till half past six the next morning, when I found we were lying at a wharf in Chicago river, having arrived about 11 the night before. Chicago is 348 miles from Mackinaw.

SUNDAY 22D

The captain of the *Buffalo* urged us to stay & breakfast on board, but the carriage we had sent for arrived & we went at once to the Tremont House, a fine large Hotel of five stories & city-like in all its furniture & appointments. Breakfasted & spent the morning on the bed trying to get rid of the effects of sea-sickness, dressed & dined. Sat in the parlor most of the afternoon. Went up into the observatory on top of the house from whence we had a very fine view of the city, the Lake & the country round. It covers a large extent of ground on both sides of the river from the Lake, & contains 40,000 inhabitants, having increased 10,000 in the last year. It is perfectly level & the country back as far as the eye can see is an extended prairie, level as a house floor. This reminds me that we had prairie chickens & hens for breakfast & dinner. They taste very much like partridges.

From our elevated position we could see the lower & opposite shore of Lake Michigan here 40 miles wide. We afterward took a walk through Michigan Av, planted with trees on the shore of the Lake, & built with pretty houses & gardens fronting the water. The streets & side walks of all the principal streets are planked instead of paved.[4] Here is also a public square laid out, but it looked neglected & loafers were sitting on the fence all around it. There are a great many trees planted in the pleasantest part of the city & it looks very pleasant. It looks singularly to see the masts of vessels among the chimneys, as the narrow river winds among the houses. There is also a canal & rail road commencing here.[5]

Took tea & spent the evening walking through the extensive parlour talking with Mrs. Twining.

---

4. The polluted Chicago River drained poorly and the level land made mud. The city was unhealthy. Six hundred and fifty people died of cholera in 1852. Planked sidewalks kept foot traffic out of the mud.
5. The Illinois and Michigan Canal from Chicago to the Illinois River, a Mississippi River tributary, completed an inland waterway from New York to New Orleans. Within a year, five railroads spread east, west, north, and south from Chicago.

CHAPTER 8

"Presenting New Beauties"
AUGUST 23–AUGUST 25, GALENA

MONDAY 23D

At 7-1/2 left on the Galena & Chicago Union Rail road[1] for Rockford on Rock river, which is at present the terminus of the road, which we reached at One O'clock. Passed through a number of small places, the principle of which are Elgin on the north fork of the Illinois, & Belvidere [*sic*] on a branch of the Rock river, both on each side of the river & pleasant looking, thriving towns.

All of this part of Illinois, & I believe most of the state is an extensive prairie, sometimes a dead level as far as the eye can reach with occasional patches of timber chiefly Oak, or gently undulating or what is called a rolling prairie with very few houses, & mostly in its natural state, covered with coarse grass, & wild flowers.

We got into a stage at Rockford, which took us to a dirty tavern where we got a miserable dinner, & afterwards we (the rail road passengers) were packed in five stages, 9 to each & started off for Galena, a distance of 82 miles. It is 167 from Chicago to Galena.

The day was intensely hot & we suffered exceedingly from heat & crowding. I rode all the way on the middle seat with two gentlemen. There was a magnificent sun set. The sun going down behind the level prairie as at sea, & the sky was filled with the most

---

1. The first railroad built in Chicago. It began operating in 1848 to bring prairie produce to Chicago for reshipping to eastern markets. By 1852 the Galena & Chicago Union also carried passengers but its tracks only reached about half way to Galena.

gorgeous colours for some time after varied by flashes of lightning which were the commencement of a storm overtaking us from the north east. In one place we saw the prairie on fire, the fire rolling along the ground & spreading to the west.

We continued on to Freeport, which place we reached about half past eight, after a violent thunder shower which flooded the roads making them in many places slippery as glass, & difficult for the horses to go faster than a walk. Here we had a wretched supper & again started in the dampness & darkness. We went miserably slow, & at last the moon came out & showed us a desolate & apparently a trackless waste with no sign of tree or life in all its extent.

Stopped occasionally to water & change horses. At most of the places, got out but in the darkness, could see but little. Passed a painful night, occasionally dosing [sic] & bumping my head against the side of the coach. Richard lost his hat while asleep, & got his cap out of his trunk at the next stopping place. Was delighted to see the sun rise on—

TUESDAY, 24TH

Stopped about seven & got breakfast at a roadside inn, & poor enough it was. Continued on arriving at Galena about 12 O'clock, putting up at the Bradley House.

As you approach the town the rolling ground rises into hills, & the country becomes very beautiful and picturesque. We saw a number of places where the reddish yellow soil had been turned up looking for lead, & passed one or two shafts & smelting furnaces. The weather was very warm & we were exceedingly uncomfortable in rooms without a breath of air, dined & slept an hour, wrote 'till tea. Directly after tea took a walk to the cliffs with Richard & a Mr. Waterman[2] a clergyman boarding in the house.

The town is built on both sides of Fever River (a corruption of Le Fievre from an early French settler), which is narrow & canal like in appearance although navigable for steam boats to the town, which is seven miles from the Mississippi. The land rises on both sides, & the streets are cut three or four deep on the steep sides of the cliffs. The gardens are generally terraced & when a little more

---

2. The Reverend T. T. Waterman, pastor at the Presbyterian Church.

improved will have a pretty effect. The rocks which project in different places have the same porous water worn appearance as at Mackinaw. One of them, or rather a cluster of them looks like a natural fort, & was fortified in the Black Hawk war.

It was a very beautiful scene after sunset. The clouds were gorgeous in the richest as well as softest tints, & the hills rising steeply on all sides with the deep & winding river were all lovely in the extreme.

The inhabitants seem to be fond of placing their houses on the highest most inconvenient points of access, & on our descent we went down over a hundred & fifty steps to get to the main street. We entered our hotel through a door on the second floor, in a back street. It was very warm & I undressed at once & retired.

WEDNESDAY 25TH

Breakfasted & took Richards to him in bed. Arranged the trunks & went shopping with Mrs. Twining. Wrote, dined, read all the afternoon. After tea, or about seven O'clock, we were told that the steamer for St. Paul was about starting.

Went on board the boat, the *Dr. Franklin*,[3] & sat on the guards till 9 O'clock, when she started. We were some time getting under way, as the river was extremely narrow & moreover obstructed by another steamboat & a boat or two which we almost ran into the opposite bank getting round, the wheels at each revolution stirring up the mud. There is a bridge building just below the town with stone abutments in the river leaving a very narrow passage for boats. Saw Joe Davis' county seat[4] which looked in the moonlight solitary enough. It is on the south side of the river just below the city.

---

3. An experienced 156-foot long wooden side-wheel packet with a long history on the Mississippi. In 1848 the Army had contracted *Dr. Franklin*'s Captain M. W. Lodwick to remove two thousand reluctant Winnebago to Minnesota. Thereafter, *Dr. Franklin* carried federal troops to their posts, cattle to feed the troops, Native Americans to treaty conferences, and government annuities to the river tribes. *Dr. Franklin* also did a boisterous business bringing tools, foodstuffs, guns, whiskey, and other frontier necessities to rival fur-trading and lead-mining companies. The fare for the four-day ride was $3.10 each plus meals. Within two years *Dr. Franklin* collided with the *Galena* and sank.
4. The courthouse on Bench Street.

It is seven miles from Galena to the Mississippi River, & the river winds continually between romantic & mostly thickly wooded banks. There is a succession of rounded hills on the south each sudden turn presenting new beauties. Although it was moon light, the air was hazy & I could not see quite as well as under different circumstances, still I saw that it was beautiful & sat up till after 12 O'clock, to see it enter the Mississippi.

The scenery was enchanting & I was well paid for my perseverance. I stood for two hours alone on the upper deck to lose nothing of the view uncertain as it was. Directly after we got into the river, the moon came out in all her splendour & showed us a beautiful wide expanse of water smooth as glass, with rather low, but green & leafy shores, & the engine which 'till then had given but feeble puffs winding slowly through the intricate navigation of Fever river, now came out in all its high pressure noise & bustle, shaking our very souls within us, & I went to bed feeling that I was indeed on the father of waters, & had turned over a new leaf in my existence.

CHAPTER 9

"Imps of Satan"
AUGUST 26–AUGUST 29, UPPER MISSISSIPPI RIVER

THURSDAY 26TH

Breakfasted & spent the morning viewing the scenery & occasionally reading a few lines from Chambers Pocket Miscellany. The river is wide & contains many Islands & sand spits. The channel is tortuous & the water at this season of the year very low. On the western shore the hills rise abruptly from the waters edge in a succession of rounded summits with tall trees & picturesque rocks appearing here & there with a fine effect. The eastern shore low with trees & the range of hills back.

At 10-1/2 stopped at Cassville a little place of about 30 houses, built on the shore, with curious round hills bare & rocky rising immediately back, or about half a mile off. The most conspicuous house was a large brick hotel. I could not help wondering if it had ever been filled with guests, as it looked any thing but inviting.

There was a curious smell & we were told that the boat had been on fire, but that it was a common occurrence & of no account.

The Turkey river here comes in from the west, but there were so many Islands with narrow channels between that I could not tell which it was. We were two or three hours aground on a sand bank but after many strenuous efforts succeeded in getting off just after dinner.

Stopped at a little place called Prairie La Porte which stood on a level high land backed by a long range of bluffs, afterwards a little town in an opening between hills called Crater town, has a landing with a road leading through a gorge in the bluffs called

McGregor's landing. Just after tea stopped at Prairie du Chien which, with Fort Crawford[1] at its southern extremity, looked beautifully in the uncertain light. It is situated much like Prairie La Port on level ground with mountains for a background only not as high, & it is said to be unhealthy.

A few miles below we saw the mouth of Wisconsin River, which looked low & full of sand banks. The river continues full of Island[s], bounded on each side by lofty bluffs or evenly rounded hills joining each other & beautifully wooded. Sometimes rising directly from the water & sometimes far inland. You can no where see more than three miles in any direction, the river winds so much. The water is exceedingly low, 17 feet lower than at high water mark. Retired early.

FRIDAY 27TH

We were aground twice in the night.

Stopped soon after breakfast to wood,[2] at the foot of a high wooded envirence [*sic*] with but one house. The scenery much the same as yesterday, rather bolder with very tall trees.

About 11 O'clock landed at the commencement of a town containing now but 6 houses, on the side of a high range of hills called Wild Cat Bluff, where there was not even a foot of bare ground. The houses seemed to be arranged on a particular line of point in a row with a good space between.

When the sun shines brightly we have a beautiful rainbow in the water beside the boat, sometimes two, caused by the spray rising from the wheel at every revolution.

I had noticed our chambermaid, a coloured woman of about

---

1. Fort Crawford, built in 1816 to protect settlers and to prevent British traders from entering the Northwest Territory, became an army center during the Black Hawk War of 1832. It was abandoned in 1849.
2. Wood-burning high-pressure engines on western river steamboats consumed copious amounts of fuel and required refueling as often as twice a day. Wood was readily available along the timbered shores of the upper Mississippi. To resupply, the crew headed into the forest with axes, or the captain found a handy wood-yard. By the 1860s, cheaper coal was the preferred fuel and on the upper Mississippi, far from coal supplies, it was often mixed with wood.

fifty years, & wondered whether she was a slave. To-day a lady told me, that in her youth she was bought in New Orleans by a Dr. Rice, who lived in some small place on the river. That after living with him 17 years & having several children he died & left her free, with a comfortable property, but she being of the hard working kind prefers the life she is now living. She is a nice clever soul & I often talk to her, as she stands at her ironing table on the guards. She does all the washing & ironing for the boat.

This morning a large Buffalo fish was caught by the wheel & thrown into the yawl towed behind the boat. It weighed 25 pounds.

Just before dinner we stopped at La Crosse, finely located on a high strip of Prairie with a high & splendid range of even rock tipped hills behind the town. Just above the river Prairie á la Crosse comes in, both on the eastern side.

The bluffs on both sides are very high, some of them over 500 feet, generally thickly wooded at the foot with smooth green declivities, often precipitous & curious highly coloured water worn rocks projecting like layers of mason work near the summit. There is a constant succession of them & where the front range opens others are discovered beyond.

The river since we entered it has been every where very wide full of green Islands & sand spits. In some places as we go along we stir up the mud & can feel the bottom of the boat grating over the bed of the river. In one place this afternoon the hills seemed to rest upon dark stone pillars worn round & in grooves by the water with their projecting capitals, appearing as though carved with the chisel.

SATURDAY 28TH

This forenoon sailed through the broad clear expanse of Lake Pepin. In one place it is five miles wide. The shores present a succession of hills divided at short intervals, but instead of the tops being rounded, they are straight having the appearance of being the termination of table lands. The Maiden's Leap, to which is attached a love legend is 500 feet high & very picturesque, the top appearing fortified & sparsely covered with tall trees.

The next object of interest was the Red Wing village, belonging to the Sioux Indians of about 30 lodges. We ran on shore directly opposite to wood, & a number of canoe loads came over, some of the men came on board to get a drink.[3] One of them had his face blackened & was perfectly frightful. They were wrapped in their blankets, & most of them tall finely formed men. The boys amused us by shooting with bows & arrows at a mark, at which they were very expert.[4]

There seemed to be a profusion of small wild grapes in the neighborhood, for almost every one who went on shore brought some on board. They were very sour & astringent in taste. Scenery all day very beautiful with miriads [sic] of lovely shady Islands.

Last night as we were aground on a sand bank, after crashing through the trees of the shore, we were obliged to have a fire kindled on the shore. There was such a fog, we could not see where we were going.

A little before five O'clock PM we reached the mouth of St Croix river. Directly at the point of juncture is a little place called Point Douglas. We went 28 miles up this river to Stillwater. We did not see much of it, as the moon was obscured, but it seemed a pleasant place with fine scenery all around. On the way we stopped at Willow River which was much smaller. Retired about 10 O'clock.

SUNDAY 29TH

Just before breakfast passed the Indian village of Little Crow, 50 lodges, also of the Sioux.[5]

Saw a number of them about. Several squaws ran down to the water to secure the canoes, which were tossed by the commotion caused by our paddle wheels. Not a great while after we ran aground close to an encampment of 22 wigwams of Buffalo skins. There were a great many children & a number of horses & dogs. We were informed that most of the men had gone on a hunting

3. The Sioux at Red Wing village called the *Dr. Franklin* "Great Medicine."
4. Emulating their ancestors, these boys were training to be hunters and warriors. On August 17, 1862, almost ten years to the day, bands of militant Sioux killed hundreds of Minnesota settlers in the fighting known as the Great Sioux Uprising.
5. Little Crow was a respected local chief who advocated peace when tribal leaders disagreed over how to deal with settlers, soldiers, and missing money. During the 1862 Great Sioux Uprising, Little Crow's son led eight hundred Sioux fighters in an attack against Fort Ridgely, on the Minnesota River.

expedition. We saw five or six only. We watched their goings & comings for an hour or more, & formed a very good idea of savage economy.

Several went off on horseback & a canoe was sent off in a very original manner. Some blankets were folded & laid upon the horse's back. Then the two front ends of a wicker frame rested upon each side of the back bone, the other end dragging on the ground. Upon this the canoe was tied & with an Indian at the horse's head they started through the woods. It came off once & they replaced it by the assistance of two or three who ran from the encampment, & if they persisted in going over many such enormous trunks of fallen trees as when they began, I presume it was a job often repeated.

The children look like young imps of Satan. They waded in & out of the water at their pleasure but little impeded by their one garment which only reached just below the hips, or laid flat upon their bellies, looking at us on the sand heaps like frogs.

(I forgot in speaking of the Indian Village of Little Crow to mention their graves which were upon the top of the hills behind the village, where the dead seemed to be wrapped in skins & placed upon an elevated staging with a small white flag to each. We saw three of these graves at this place.

At this village the Captain put one of the coloured waiters ashore for misbehavior.)[6]

---

6. A common punishment for misdeeds aboard a steamship. Many Captains were not particular about where they dropped offenders—on docks, sand bars, remote shores, or islands. [The editor moved this parenthetical section from its original location following the next paragraph.]

CHAPTER 10

"Beautifully Situated"

AUGUST 30–AUGUST 31, ST. PAUL AND
ST. ANTHONY

SUNDAY, 29TH [CONTINUED]

At last we got over this the worst bar we had yet incountered [*sic*],
& in three more miles reached St Pauls, [*sic*] the capitol of Minnesota.[1] There are some singular bluffs just before reaching the city
& on the same side of the river, the east. We went up a steep road
into the town which is built high above the river in the same way I
have mentioned before with a range of hills back. It seems flourishing & contains 3000 inhabitants. We went to the American Hotel[2]
in St Anthony street which is the principle thoroughfare.

---

1. In 1837 a disreputable Canadian voyageur named Pierre "Old Pig's Eye"
   Parrant won a footrace to claim land near a bend in the Mississippi nine miles
   downstream from the Falls of St. Anthony. A settlement there of Canadian
   refugees ejected from Fort Snelling's reserve was called "Pig's Eye" until
   Parrant sold his claim for thirty dollars. Father L. Gautier then built a log
   church there in 1840 and decided that the apostle Paul had been slighted in
   naming the local sites. The U.S. government created the Minnesota Territory
   in 1849 when Iowa and Wisconsin became states, naming St. Paul the territorial capitol. Abundant waterpower, established trading posts, and river com-
   munication with the rest of the United States drew settlers to the area. From
   1850 to 1852 the Minnesota territorial population grew from 6,077 to 20,000.
2. The American House "was a hotel par excellence for the times, [but] the floor
   was made of splintered, unplaned boards. . . . The furniture of the bedroom
   consisted of a bed and a wash stand" (Lucy L. W Morris, ed. *Old Rail Fence
   Corners: Frontier Tales Told by Minnesota Pioneers* [St. Paul: Minnesota
   Historical Society Press, 1976], 157).

After church a party of officers & ladies from Fort Snelling came into the parlour. They stayed & dined afterward going off in a large open waggon drawn by four mules & driven by a dragoon.[3] Just before dinner took a short walk with Richard to get an idea of the place.[4]

Met two tall Indians with scarlet blankets & leggings & rifles & powderhornes, looking quite stately.

Wrote & sat in the parlour conversing with two ladies who had lived in the Indian country. One a Mrs. Bradley wife of a non-commissioned officer at Fort Gaines.[5] The other wife of an Indian agent a long way up the country. Took tea & while Mrs. Twining went to church, spent the evening talking to two gentlemen in the parlour, & retired at half past ten.

MONDAY 30TH

When we arose this morning it was raining quite fast, but soon after breakfast it cleared off & was bright & pleasant all day. About half past eight we started in a pleasant light covered carriage with a driver (Harrison Kelly)[6] leaving our trunks behind us, for the Falls of St Anthony, 9 miles off & 2087 miles from the Gulf of Mexico. Our road was mostly over level prairie land with Oaks scattered along most of our way.

We stopped at a house of refreshment about half way, where were several Sioux lounging about. One of them had a tomihawk [sic] in his hand which he sold me. They were as most of their tribe tall with fine figures, & this one very good looking.

Soon after we stopped at an Indian Lodge where a baby was sitting on the floor. I sent the driver to bring it to me. The mother,

---

3. An army calvary soldier.
4. The Falls of St. Anthony just upstream interrupted further river travel north. Three small frontier towns clustered around the junction of the St. Peters and Mississippi rivers: St. Paul on the eastern Mississippi riverbank; St. Anthony farther upstream; and Mendota, a trading post on the St. Peters River, to the west. The domineering Fort Snelling, built of stone, stood on the western bluff above the river junction.
5. Built in 1848 farther up the Mississippi to enforce Indian policies.
6. Willoughby & Powers' livery furnished carriages for visitors for $3.75. Harrison Kelly was a twenty-four-year-old carpenter born in New York.

a good looking squaw, brought it to the carriage & I took it on my lap. It was very fat but frightfully dirty. Around its neck was a string of red beads with some bear's claws & curious bits of metal for "charms." We tried to make signs to the mother to find out how old it was, & I held up some fingers. She thought we wanted to buy it & looked the picture of consternation. At last however we made her comprehend & found it was six months old.

We drove at once to the Falls. They are divided into three parts. We approached on the eastern side, where lies the City of St. Anthony.[7] The oldest place in the territory it contains 2500 inhabitants. The first part is low sloping off in rapids. We forded the river [Mississippi] a little way above them to an Island over a smooth rocky bottom. We then got out of the carriage & walked across to the other side where we had a fine view of the middle Fall upon a level with it but looking up the river, as at table rock Niagara.

It is 40 feet in height & very beautiful. It is a scene of the wildest confusion. There seems to have been some grand convulsion of natur [sic] which has split the rocks & strewn them over the bed of the river in immense slabs of from one to five or six feet thick, with as smooth surface as though cut by man & in all positions. Some of them standing erect & all kinds of positions. Added to this a great quantity of drift wood & timber has come down from above helping the confusion below.

We sat over an hour looking our fill at the rushing water & the beautiful rapids below. There is an Island commencing just at the fall below which impeded our view of the more western fall. The

---

7. Soldiers from Fort Snelling had built lumber mills on the western Mississippi shore at the Falls of St. Anthony. Franklin Steele built another lumber mill on the eastern side and a dam across half the river. The settlement around Steele's mill became the town of St. Anthony. "Sprawled over a lightly wooded prairie sloping gently to the river, St. Anthony at first glance looked like a New England village. . . . [But] 'Nasty piratical looking pigs' roamed at will, and streets were filled with stumps. Stagecoaches, carts, and wagons, rumbling in from St. Paul—the head of Mississippi River navigation. . . . Indians wandered through the town, strangers to the noise and bustle around them. Piles of logs and lumber from the sawmills dotted the landscape, and the whine of the saws could be heard above the roar of the falls" (Lucille M. Kane, *The Waterfall That Built a City* [St. Paul: Minnesota Historical Society, 1966], 29).

whole river here including the Islands is more than three quarters of a mile wide. We forded the river back again & drove a little below where I went down a steep place with Richard & the driver, where under a high hanging cliff, from which the water was constantly dripping, we procured some fine specimens of petrified moss. It was excessively warm, although there was a great deal of air stirring.

Went to the St. Charles House[8] & dined, & after dinner, started off again to visit the western fall.

We crossed a high bridge, & the wind blew so hard that I thought it would have carried us over into the rapids, onto the island expecting to take the Ferry[9] across to the shore, but the ferryman who was an exceedingly handsome man, refused to take us over as he said in such a high wind, the loss of carriage and horses was certain. It was worked by ropes fastened on each side & was quite intricate.

We then rode two miles farther down, where we were taken across on the most curious contrivance I ever saw. The boat was just large enough for the carriage & was worked by the current, chains & ropes being fastened to four boats anchored in the river above.

The road for a short distance on the other side was very bad, until we ascended the cliff to the table land or extensive prairie above. All below the Falls the banks are rocky & precipitous with in many places perpendicular cliffs of very singular appearance, but above, as far as we could see, the banks were low & green to the waters edge with Islands as further down. The Western Fall comprises about two thirds of the whole & is very grand & beautiful. It has the same wild chaotic appearance & the roar is deep & thunder-like as Niagara. We could have gazed forever but were obliged to hurry away.

Our road led for five miles over a level & sometimes gently rolling prairie with a green skirting of trees in the horizon to the two

8. The St. Charles Hotel on Marshall Street, called by one 1852 resident the "old" hotel, had twenty beds in one room upstairs.

9. The army offered free ferry service above the Falls of St. Anthony. Most Minnesota ferries were locally made, simple flat boats with side rails and a ramp on either end. John Tapper, a thirty-year-old Englishman, was the St. Anthony's ferryman for years.

beautiful little Lakes of Calhoun & Harriet.[10] They are about 3 miles long & nearly as broad with beautifully sloping green wooded shores & a deep sparkling wave. Today they were quite rough. On the shores of the latter we picked up some small carnelians & agates.

On our way back to the hotel at St Anthony we rode through the town, which is beautifully situated on a level prairie looking down upon the river & commanding a fine wide prospect all around. It contains [blank space] inhabitants. Took a late tea & retired soon after.

At St Pauls we saw a number of Indians whose land is on the opposite side of the river, & two of them on horseback, in all the bravery or Savage costume. They most of them use red paint lavishly on their heads & faces.

Near the Hotel, there is a tame bear, black & with very thick hair, it was caught young & is now over a year old.

TUESDAY 31ST

Directly after breakfasted [sic] started in the carriage for the Little Falls[11] on Little Falls creek. The fall is about 25 feet wide at top & 60 feet high. The rock under the fall was worn so that it shelved under in a semicircle & the ravine through which the stream passed off in rapids to the Mississippi was very romantic & picturesque.

We gathered some wild flowers & rushes & passed on to the Fort.[12] On our way we saw large flocks of Blackbirds, which often alighted in the fields & on the trees quite near us.

---

10. Lake Harriet was named for the wife of Lieutenant Colonel Henry Leavenworth, Fort Snelling's designer, and Lake Calhoun for the politician John C. Calhoun.

11. First called Brown's Falls and later Little Falls, about 1852 it permanently acquired the wonderful name "Minnehaha," or the "Laughing Waters." In 1855, Henry Wadsworth Longfellow made Minnehaha Falls famous in his "Song of Hiawatha."

12. Fort Snelling dominated 120-foot-high bluffs on the west bank of the Mississippi. Completed in 1824, the diamond-shaped fortress with ten-foot barricades and corner towers had formed a link in a chain of forts from the Great Lakes to the Missouri River to protect Americans from the British, Spanish, French, and Sioux. The great fort had never seen battle. When the

Fort Snelling is situated at the junction of the Mississippi &
St. Peters[13] rivers, on the north side, & in the southern point, is the
town of Mendota or St Peters which is quite small & stands high
with hills rising behind. The Fort is built of stone & very extensive
& substantial. There are now stationed here 2 companies of
infantry & one of Dragoons. Richard went through the stable to
see their horses, which are all fine animals. They have extensive
vegetable gardens in fine order, with the tents of the gardeners
interspersed. It stands on a high rock which terminates a wide
prairie, around which a road is cut down to the ferry which we
crossed in a boat of the same construction as the one mentioned
before, & there is a fine road now finishing winding up the side of
the cliff on the eastern side. The government or military reserve
here is ten miles square.

We had a very pleasant ride of three or four miles through a
country mostly level to the edge of a steep ravine, where we alighted & winding our way down & through it about two hundred feet
we reached the entrance of a cave[14] formed in the side of a hill in a
soft white sandstone with a cold & clear stream running through it.
It was wet & after going a little way so dark that I could see nothing. So putting on my over shoes & trying to make some bushes
burn I left the first large room & was just picking my way through
a narrow passage where the stream occupied nearly all the flooring,
when my light went out & I was left in darkness, of course. I was
obliged to retrace my steps. But it was exceedingly tantalizing, as
there is still a large apartment beyond beside a long passage. We
entirely forgot to bring candles.

Rode three miles through a pleasant wood looking away down
upon the river & the woods opposite & arrived at St Pauls just
before dinner. After dinner packed our trunks & went on board the
steamer *Martha*[15] for Galena, which started at half past Three

---

government's line of forts moved farther west in the late 1840s, Fort Snelling
became a supply depot and sometime social center.

13. In 1852, Congress officially named this the Minnesota River.

14. There were several caves on the eastern Mississippi shore. This is probably
Fountain Cave, so named because a brook issues from its mouth like a foun-
tain. Spring Cave (possibly another name for Fountain Cave) and Carver's
Cave also attracted visitors.

15. A 180-ton side-wheeler built in Pennsylvania in 1849.

O'clock. We made good progress as this boat draws much less water than the other.

The Indian encampment we noticed going up was gone with nothing left but the poles of the wigwams & the remains of their fires.

As I described every thing so particularly going up there is but little to note now. The table is very poor, every thing brought on the table cold & butter miserable. Retired very early.

CHAPTER 11

"A Good Stateroom"

SEPTEMBER 1–SEPTEMBER 11, MISSISSIPPI RIVER AND ST. LOUIS

WEDNESDAY SEPT 1ST

It was cloudy when we rose & about Ten began to rain, which it did all day with occasional thunder & lightning. Some very severe. Just after Eleven we passed the steamer *Nominee*[1] on her way up.

Everything looked beautifully green, particularly the vines which festoon from the branches of the trees concealing entirely the trunk in their green embrace.

Last night there was a great deal of noise on board with crashing of branches, & as we had the end state room so poorly built that we could see the moonlight through the cracks, I was somewhat troubled lest the thin partition should be torn off & we be lying in the open air. Beside this the Captain saw fit to wood at midnight, & running up into the woods, we were boarded by myriads of Mosquitoes who gave us no more peace.

At the far end of the saloon there was gambling all the evening with cards, in which all the men seemed to be highly interested. Retired at 8 1/2.

---

1. A 212-ton side-wheel ship originally built in 1848 for the Pittsburgh-Cincinnati trade. In April 1850, *Nominee* was one of the first two Galena & Minnesota Packet Company steamers to navigate to St. Paul. She thereafter ran regularly between St. Paul and Galena until she snagged and was lost in 1854.

THURSDAY 2D

About half past eight entered Fever river & soon after came upon the *Danube* steamer which had just been snagged & was sinking above her lower deck.[2] We took off her passengers, among whom were three women & two children.

Soon after we passed the *Jenny Lind*[3] going out. We passed over another boat to the wharf & found ourselves at the American House about Eleven O'clock. Read a little & dined. After dinner we took a carriage & black driver & went to Dubuque,[4] 16 miles.

The road was in general hilly & in the highest parts commanded an extensive prospect of hills & woodlands & cultivated fields. We passed a Jesuit College & little church built of light yellow stone with numerous out buildings & pleasant grounds & gardens of vegetables. In the course of our drive we were in Illinois, Wisconsin & Iowa. Crossed the river on a steam ferry boat to a large Island in company with a stage & two other carriages. Across this island we rode & again a ferry of the same simple construction as those at St. Pauls. It was after Six when we arrived at the City Hotel Dubuque.

Soon after tea, which was immediately prepared for us, retired.

FRIDAY 3D

Rose early & wrote before breakfast. There were punkahs[5] arranged down through the center of the room over the breakfast table which a boy constantly agitated keeping up a current of air, & the dishes clear of flies. A very good house & very reasonable in all charges.[6] At Eight O'clock we started in the carriage to visit one of the lead

---

2. Four days later, the *Danube* struck rocks at Port Byron, Illinois, sank, and was lost.
3. The *Jenny Lind*'s uniquely designed extra-wide forward hull was supposed to protect her delicate paddle wheels from rocks, floating logs, debris, and other obstructions.
4. Dubuque, on the western bank of the river, was growing rapidly. Streets were being paved and the harbor improved. One hundred new buildings, mostly brick, rose in 1852. By the end of the year the city's population reached seven thousand.
5. Large canvas-covered fan suspended from the ceiling, operated by a cord.
6. The total bill for two at Dubuque was $2.75.

"diggings" as they are called here.[7] Passed through a good part of the town which is pleasant & contains 6000 inhabitants. The channel of the river is here very narrow with Islands low & green.

The lead mine we went to visit is two miles north west of Dubuque & the road is good, though hilly. We found a little covered shed under which a horse walked round working the ropes on a wheel which lowered & brought up buckets from below. The shaft or opening was near at hand. Mrs. Twining & I were lowered together, standing facing each other in the bucket, & holding on to the rope first taking off our bonnets & tying our handkerchiefs round our heads. Richard was lowered afterwards. The descent was 125 feet perpendicular & we landed in a high cavern with a dark pool of water 10 feet deep before us, running off in a little stream into darkness, & water trickling on all sides some of it on our heads. Here a man gave each of us a candle & led the way to the east through a narrow passage with a small car & train way in the middle. The car he pushed before him for about two hundred feet when we left the lower passage & climbed into an upper drift through which we continued our way three hundred feet farther, making in all 500 feet of progress horizontally in the bowels of the earth.

In this upper passage we found a miner & two women visitors, & we here procured some fine specimens of ore & spar.[8] The passages are mostly the natural winding ways of subterranean caves widened & extended upwards or downwards, as the ore required. In some places we had to stoop very low to get along & in others the rock touched us on both sides. Again it would shelve off so that one could scarcely see the extent standing on tiptoe & sometimes it would be as much as 20 feet high.

The appearance of the rock in many places gave the idea of insecurity from the great seams & over hanging points. There were remains of stalactites in some parts & one of the miners with a hammer & chisel got us off the best that were left. The ore is mostly

7. Almost seventy-five years earlier, a French pioneer, Julien Dubuque, had operated lead mines called the "Mines of Spain" on Mesquakie tribal land. After the Black Hawk War, the Mesquakie ceded their land and the lead mines to the United States. In 1852, Dubuque's lead mines shipped 8,700 tons of lead valued at $348,000, more than double the previous year.
8. Feldspar, a crystalline, nonmetallic mineral.

mixed with earth which is loosened with pickaxes. The passages were slippery with a kind of wet clay, & the air cool & pleasant. We again got into our bucket & were not sorry to feel the warm sunlight of the upper air. We saw but three workmen & they did not seem to be doing much.

We got back to the Hotel about Eleven & after a nice lunch of beef steak, tea & apple pie we started for Galena. Our polite landlord Mr. Hewit putting us in the carriage. We again crossed the ferries, the little *Utah* puffing intensely, & after a very warm ride over pretty rough roads, arrived at our Hotel in Galena about half past four. Read, took tea & wrote. Retired at half past Eight.

SATURDAY 4TH

A warm day. Read & walked about town some, going into several shops.

Have come to the conclusion that Galena is the most vulgar stupid dirty & uninteresting place I ever saw.[9]

There is no steamer in for St Louis, so we cannot get away, retired at 8 1/2.

SUNDAY 5TH

After breakfast Richard went to the water & found four steamers had come in among them one for St Louis. He secured us a good stateroom.

Did not go out all day. Our windows look out upon a side street, & our prospect is the side door of a rum hole & an extensive livery stable. We have seen a great deal of intemperance & any quantity of rowdyism. It seems as though no man through all this western country can speak without an oath. This Hotel is like almost all western hotels, dreadfully noisy. All today they have been singing & whistling all sorts of tunes & the piano has been going

---

9. Galena's population had grown on traffic to and from the lead mines. But when railroads bridged the river to Dubuque, Iowa, and reached other river ports in the next several years, much of the commerce in lead and mining supplies deserted Galena.

all the afternoon. Gracias a Dios,[10] we hope to be off tomorrow morning, retired early under the first mosquito curtain I ever slept under.

MONDAY 6TH

As we were told that the steamer *Minnesota*[11] would leave this morning at 9 O'clock we went on board, but she lay in the river all day taking in freight & did not start till 6 O'clock P.M. We made but little progress in the night, morning finding us opposite the town of Huntsville.

We found the beds so full of bed bugs that it was impossible to sleep, & after killing one cockroach also, I did not attempt it. We went out into the saloon, Mrs. Twining taking possession of an old tabouret[12] & I reclining in a rocking chair. As can be imagined we passed a wretched night, & slept but little.

The scenery becomes somewhat tame immediately after leaving Fever River. The banks are low & wooded, & country houses & fields of corn, etc. more frequent.

TUESDAY 7TH

We complained of the bugs this morning to the chambermaid, a slovenly girl of about 19 years, & she said "it was no use to do any thing, it would only disturb them & make them wild."

We got along very slowly, & were most of the day on the rapids, which are between Albany & Rock Island, & are 16 miles long.

The water is now so low that it is exceedingly difficult to get over them. We had two heavily laden barges[13] with us which, at the commencement of the rapids, were provided with sweeps, or long oars, & set adrift. These got on the rocks & we after passing the worst part, were obliged to go back & get them off. Several times we struck so hard on the rocks that everything rattled, & it needed

10. Thank God! or Thanks be to God!
11. A 149-ton side-wheel boat built in 1849 for the Northern Line.
12. A cylindrical seat or stool without back or arms.
13. Steamers sometimes towed barges loaded with freight.

the full power of the machinery to drag us scraping over them most disagreeably. We lay by all night at a little place on the rapids.

What sleep I had was on three chairs in the saloon. Richard laid on the floor in the gentlemen's saloon. Mrs. Twining again took possession of her settee. The carpenters were at work on board all night, & there were several babies who, helped by a yelping dog on deck, kept up a constant uproar all night.

They have been pumping occasionally ever since we started, & altogether I never was in such an uncomfortable place.

WEDNESDAY 8TH

Started soon after light, & after a few drags on the rocks got over the rapids & to the shore at Davenport before breakfast. This is a very pretty place in Iowa; larger & pleasanter than any we have yet seen on the Mississippi. It is directly opposite Rock Island, which is Three miles long & a mile & a half broad. The upper end is green & pretty with here & there a scattered house. The handsome residence of Colonel Davenport who was here murdered July 4th 1845 is here just above Fort Armstrong which is in the center of the Island twenty feet above the water.[14] It looks old & in ruin & is entirely deserted. It is quite picturesque & adds much to the scene. The lower end of the Island is thickly built & as large as Davenport opposite.

Here we took in a number of passengers, & all from the *Danube* which we passed sunk up the river. We also passed the *Jenny Lind* fast on the rocks of the rapids.

Read most of the day in the course of which passed several nucleus for towns with high sounding names but of little apparent pretensions, among which Muscatine (formerly Bloomington) beautifully situated on the Iowa shore, mounting back upon the cliffs, & Burlington the former capitol of Iowa, & the burial place of the Indian chief Black Hawk were about the only ones very noticeable.

One more dreadful night on board. We had beds made up on

---

14. U.S. Army Colonel George Davenport established Fort Armstrong in 1816 to help control Native Americans and British traders. Its stone and timber blockhouses and magazine, used in the Black Hawk War, were abandoned in 1836.

the floor of the saloon, & it was covered, as we took on a great many passengers on our way. I threw myself clothes & all upon a mattress & slept as well as I could with a child's feet on my head & two women on my feet all night.

Thursday 9th

Found on wakening that we were stationary at the little town of Montrose, & directly opposite the old famous Mormon city of Nauvoo, at the head of the Des Moines Rapids. Nauvoo is splendidly situated on the eastern shore, on a "bluff" sloping from the water to a great height ending in a tableland & once contained a population of 18000, & many handsome buildings. High above all towered brilliant in the rising sun light the ruin of the famous Temple, destroyed by fire kindled by a mob October 9th 1848. It is of white marble & has been purchased by the French Catholics to erect upon the ruins a catholic seminary. Even in its ruin the city was very beautiful & the scene highly picturesque.

There is an Island directly between it & Montrose which prevents a good view until you get a mile or two below, where for several more it is very fine.

We took a breakfast on board at 6 O'clock, & embarked with some 25 other passengers (most of the gentlemen preferring the stage) on board the flat boat *Paul Jones* towed by a horse for Keokuk below the rapids a distance of 12 miles. The middle part of the boat was covered, with openings in the sides, & we were very comfortably accommodated with seats or benches & our trunks, which were piled up in the middle. The captain was a pleasant plain old man who gave us watermelon & apples & seemed very good natured & obliging. Flat as we were we grounded on the rocks several times, & the horse was wading up to his body & over half of the time in the middle of the river instead of the shore. The river was generally as wide as the Hudson opposite New York.

At Keokuk we went on board the Steamer *Belle Gould*[15] for St Louis. She was new & beautifully decorated. We had a very nice

---

15. The two-hundred-foot-long *Belle Gould* was built earlier in the year at New Albany, Indiana, for the St. Louis–Keokuk trade. After two years on the river she snagged near Cairo and was lost.

stateroom & were once more comfortable.

Saw the mouth of the Des Moines, which was a narrow stream entering the river opposite the pretty little town of Warsaw. Quincy in Illinois is situated on an elevation of 125 feet, with a steep slope to the river & is a very beautiful & flourishing town. It has some 7000 inhabitants. Hannibal in Missouri is very finely located between lofty bluffs on a plain bounded by hills in the distance & appeared very pleasant from the water. It is quite large & growing rapidly. The last of our views this day was a dusky one of [the town of] Louisiana on the western shore, but it was too dark to see more than a long line of lights above a high & steep levee. The western shore all day has been very beautiful with occasional bluffs, which reminded us of Lake Pepin, & a great many Islands.

I had not undressed for three days & had a delightful night of rest "comme il faut."[16]

FRIDAY 10TH

Went out on the guards this morning a half hour before we arrived at Alton Illinois. The Illinois shore was high & of the same character as the upper Mississippi, & the city itself large & flourishing, & handsomely built for the most part of brick or stone. Just before breakfast we saw the mouth of the Missouri, which rolls in among low sand banks a yellow muddy flood imparting its peculiar colour to the river ever after, which before was about the clearness of the Hudson.

The shores on both sides low & cheerless & in high water must be entirely overflowed for miles. Sometimes it (the river here) is thirty miles wide.

Just before 9 O'clock we arrived at St Louis[17] & sent Richard

---

16. As one should.
17. Philip Hone described the St. Louis waterfront: "Fifty large steamboats, at least, lie head on, taking in and discharging their cargoes. . . . The whole of the levee is covered, as far as the eye can see, with merchandise landed or to be shipped; thousands of barrels of flour and bags of corn, hogsheads of tobacco, and immense piles of lead (one of the great staples), whilst foreign merchandise and the products of the lower country are carried away to be lodged in the stores which form the front of the city" (quoted in Margaret A.

to the shore for Alfred Lee,[18] who soon came & went with us to the Monroe House on Second Street.

At Ten O'clock went in a carriage with Alfred, Mrs. Twining, Richard & a Mrs. Barger (a lady of St. Louis whose acquaintance we made on the *Minnesota*) to take a ride.

We went north through the suburb called Bremen to Bellefontaine Cemetery, a beautiful a spot of 164 acres, laid out in the style of Mount Auburn & Greenwood, with a fine variety of hill & dale & lofty trees, & near the entrance a curious & picturesque cottage of stone in the Gothic style for the keeper. It is yet new, but there are several splendid monuments, & a great deal of good taste in the arrangements & decorations. On our way home we visited the Hyde Park gardens, a great resort especially on Sundays, for the citizens. Here we saw what they call a Fandango. It is a large wheel turned by a crank with 4 cars which revolve &, when at the highest point, command a fine view of the city & surrounding country.

We returned through a dusty noisy thoroughfare called Broadway which terminates in Second Street where a long market takes up the space in the middle of the street. It looks most like the Bowery[19] near 8th & 9th Streets, with country wagons standing on both sides & stores like the Bowery.

Opposite the city is an Island, now I believe connected with Illinois, about a mile & a half long, called Bloody Island, as it was formerly the Drilling ground of Missouri. It is low sandy ground with a thick growth of stunted vegetation. In the neighborhood mostly on the western side there are curious circular holes some very shallow, & others 14 or 15 feet deep, filled generally with water & seeming to come from springs, called by the people here Sinks. They have no outlets and are never stagnant. They are considered a curiosity as there are so many & of such regular form.

St Louis is large & very fast increasing; it contains now 100,000 inhabitants. The streets are generally McAdamized & in a

Christman, *1846 Portrait of the Nation* [Washington, D.C.: Smithsonian Institution Press, 1996], 57).

18. Juliette's sister, Sarah Starr, had married George Lee, an Englishman and New Orleans banker, who had died in 1849. Alfred Lee was George's son from a prior marriage.

19. A busy commercial section of New York City.

miserable condition. The Southern part contains 20,000 Germans & is very unpleasant & dirty.[20]

The most fashionable street is Olive & contains many fine residences. It is generally well & substantially built, but not healthy & very dirty.[21] There are some very large sugar refineries & a very extensive Castor Oil Factory, & also one of White lead.

After dinner, which was a scene of indescribable noise & confusion, about 200 dining at different tables in the same room. We rode to the Arsenal[22] south of the city with Mr. & Mrs. Lee. It is finely situated on the river & we went through the different workshops where they were altering the locks of muskets from flint locks to percussion, & a large building filled the three stories with artillery waggons & stores. Every thing of course was in fine order & the officers' houses very handsome; also those for the soldiers, etc. There is always a company stationed here. I should think there were as many as 12 or 15 acres inclosed [sic] in a high stone wall, with a handsome open iron railing & gate on the river side.

We went to Mr. Lee's house & spent the night, Richard sleeping at the Monroe House.

Saturday 11th

After breakfast, after walking in the garden & gathering some flower seeds Mrs. Twining, Richard, Alfred & I went shopping. There are some fine shops, well furnished & it looks like a flourish-

---

20. Founded by French fur traders in 1764, St. Louis and the Louisiana territory changed hands between the French and Spanish until France ceded it to the United States in 1804. The city's small population was almost entirely French, but as center of the western fur trade, gateway to Texas, California, and Oregon, and major steamboat port, it had drawn immigrants from the eastern United States and, lately, Ireland and Germany. By 1850 one-third the city's population was German-born.

21. May 4, 1849, three years earlier, fire had ravaged a large portion of St. Louis. That disaster was followed by a severe cholera epidemic.

22. The United States Arsenal established in 1827 was completed about 1840. At the start of the Civil War, it held the largest ammunition supply in the West. The Jefferson Barracks, since 1826 a garrison for troops serving the Mississippi River valley, were also on the grounds.

ing city. The Planters House is the most aristocratic. It is built in the style of the Astor House, but of brick.[23]

Went back to Alfred's to dinner, & at 3 O'clock left in a carriage for the Monroe House where I packed my luggage, & we went on board the Steamer *Fashion*[24] bound to Louisville, which started about half past 4 O'clock. Bid good bye to Alfred.

23. The elegant six-story, 306-room, granite Greek revival hotel built in New York by John Jacob Astor in 1836. New York's premier hotel well into the 1850s, it housed eight hundred guests around a central courtyard, each floor with bathing and toilet facilities and gas lamps. The Astor House refused admission to unescorted ladies.
24. A 149-ton side-wheel steamer about four years old.

CHAPTER 12

"Grand and Romantic Scenery"

SEPTEMBER 11–SEPTEMBER 17, OHIO RIVER AND NEW YORK

SATURDAY 11TH [CONTINUED]

The city looks larger from the water & is I believe 7 miles long on the river, but not deep from east to west. We did not go far before dark, & the boat laid to all night on a/c [account] of dangerous navigation because of low water & snags. There are more of them between St. Louis & the mouth of the Ohio than any other part of the river. The scenery is finer than above St. Louis & we saw some fine bluffs which reminded us of the Upper Mississippi.

There are not more than 6 or 8 ladies & it is quiet and pleasant. The gentlemen are numerous & of a better class than we have hitherto met.

SUNDAY 12TH

I arose early to lose none of the fine scenery which until we got past Cape Girardeau was very fine, interspersed with bluffs. Here they end & there is no more such below on the Mississippi. Saw the mouth of the Kaskaskia which is clear & pretty, though narrow. The towns of Chester & St. Genevieve are beautifully situated on high ground the former running up a high hill & apparently extending back beyond it. From there to the Ohio the river has few charms with its dirty muddy water, innumerable snags & sand banks & its ragged flat shores, covered with tall trees & sometimes only bushes.

Had a nice table of luncheon for the ladies at 11 & dinner at 2. Read all day. Just before dark we arrived at Cairo at the mouth of the Ohio river, which for 100 miles is as wide as the parent river, although its shores are prettier than the last below Galena. Cairo has not grown like many of the towns in this neighborhood on a/c of its low & unhealthy location, but its large Hotel looked well from the water.

Monday 13th

The scenery today very fine. The Illinois shore is generally high with bluffs on the river & green on both shores to the waters edge. We have not however yet lost sight of the sand banks. Directly after leaving Elizabeth, a very pretty town in Illinois, we came to Hurricane Island which is beautiful, with tall trees & verdure hanging over the river. It is two or three miles long & the narrow southern channel up which we passed was winding & pleasant. The Kentucky bank was also green & shady.

A few miles further on we saw Cave in Rock, on the Illinois side, which is a hole about 20 feet high in the bluff, facing the river, which after the distance of 200 yards, expands into a large room 30 feet high & 125 feet long. It was once the resort of a band of river banditti[1] who plundered & murdered the flat boatmen, but is now solitary.

We passed many towns, all pleasantly situated, but all new towns are so much alike that one description suffices for all.

Just at dusk we stopped at Henderson in Kentucky. Here they are extensively engaged in the Tobacco culture, & the Captain tells us it is the wealthiest town on the river. We spent most the evening on the upper deck talking with the Captain (Sherley) who is exceedingly polite & attentive to all his lady passengers. Retired a little past 9.

---

1. Bandits.

TUESDAY 14TH

The boat went much faster last night, probably the water was deeper, or fewer snags, & we were almost racked to death with the powerful machinery. We have been much amused by a party of officers in the army & the wife of one, on board. We had a pleasant little conversation with her this morning & find she is going on a visit to her friends in Maryland. Has been stationed at Fort Kearney on the Missouri & is wife to the surgeon, & has been married just 3 years. They have with them a large Newfoundland dog & two slaves, man & woman. Her name is Hammond.

The scenery has been very fine all day. The banks high & sometimes in lofty precipitous stone cliffs, & very winding with pretty towns & farm houses. We arrived at Louisville a little after dark. Just after tea, passed the pretty little town of West Point & the famous Salt River. Thought one might have a worse fate than to be "rowed up." It was narrow but the water looked clear & deep & the banks overhung with trees. Conversed all the evening with Mrs. Hammond & retired at 10 1/2.

WEDNESDAY 15TH

Were knocked up[2] this morning at 5 O'clock & breakfasted at 6 1/2. At Eight, we got into an omnibus with other passengers in a heavy rain & rode three miles through dreadful roads & the business part of Louisville to the Steamer *Lady Pike* which lay above the rapids, which impede the navigation of the Ohio past the city.

The river is here divided by a beautiful green Island with a sand bar at the head. There is a canal for steamboats, but none but small ones can use it. Louisville has 50,000 inhabitants, but owing to the rain we did not see much of it. Along the levee were fine rows of high brick stores & it seemed very busy.

The *Lady Pike* is small & dirty & we have one of the worst state rooms, but console ourselves that it is but one night. She is

---

2. Summoned by knocking on the door.

crowded with passengers of both sexes.

It rained nearly all day. Nevertheless enjoyed the scenery which is very fine, with a succession of rounded bluffs, on each side of the river alternately. Passed at Carrollton the mouth of the Kentucky river, which seemed to partake of the character of the Ohio in winding immediately out of sight. The scenery of this river higher up is said to be remarkably wild.

Sat in the Saloon 'till 9 P.M. making remarks upon the passengers & retired with many misgivings to our mean, miserable stateroom.

THURSDAY 16TH

Were knocked up at 4 O'clock & found we were lying at the levee in Cincinnati.[3] Although we were introduced particularly to the Captain & he promised to see us to the railroad himself, he was not forthcoming, & we took a carriage (after sending our baggage to the cars) & rode as much as we could through the city before following our trunks. We could see but little, but what we did see looked pleasant & well built. On a slope from the river & with every appearance of riches & prosperity. Directly opposite the city at the mouth of the Licking river is Newport where there is a U.S. garrison & Covington which has some large manufactories.

We started at Six O'clock on the Little Miami rail-road[4] for Cleveland, & about 8 breakfasted at the little town called Morrow. For a long time our course lay along the Little Miami river & was very pleasant. Passed through many little places which looked new & flourishing & among which & the largest was Xenia, on a wide plain & handsomely built. It is called one of the prettiest towns in Ohio.

About 3 O'clock we stopped to dine at Columbus, which is the capital of the state of Ohio, situated on the eastern bank of the

---

3. Cincinnati was one of the largest cities west of the Appalachian Mountains, with a population well over seventy-five thousand. A meatpacking center and a busy port on the river between Pittsburgh and New Orleans, Cincinnati boasted a theater and museum as well as land offices, churches, and markets.
4. The Little Miami Railroad recently had connected from Cincinnati to Cleveland on Lake Erie.

Scioto river. It has a population of between 14 & 15000, & has several large public buildings & the state Penitentiary, built of light stone, & which we passed on leaving the city. I did not leave the cars, not feeling very well & Richard & Mrs. Twining brought me something from the house.

Our route was principally through a level country well wooded & some of it rather swampy. In the neighborhood of Cleveland the forest was very dense & rather dreary & we could obtain no view of the city, owing to our plunging into a high sand bank just before entering the town. It is very picturesquely situated at the mouth of the Cuyahoga river on Lake Erie, & is divided into an upper & lower town. The lower is devoted principally to business, but the upper is beautifully built on heights commanding an extensive view of land & water & shaded with trees. Its population is about 15000.

Went immediately on board the Steamer *Northern Indiana*, which left soon after or at 6 O'clock for Dunkirk. She is a first class boat something like our best on the Sound,[5] & splendidly fitted up. We had 1200 passengers, & they were obliged to set the supper table six times, that all might be served. Spent the evening in the upper Saloon listening to the music. There was a piano & two gentlemen & a lady played, & a number of male voices joined in the singing. Slept in the lower cabin on the floor & was waked at two O'clock on—

FRIDAY 17TH

Soon after we arrived at Dunkirk, which is the terminus of the ~~Delaware & Hudson river~~ Erie rail-road, on Lake Erie.[6]

It was very cold & we went in an Omnibus to the Mansion

---

5. Long Island Sound off New York City and the coast of Connecticut.

6. The New York & Erie Railroad opened to its full length in May 1851, becoming the longest continuous railroad in the United States. Called the "Work of the Age," the railroad's six-foot-wide track wound through and over a succession of valleys and rivers from Lake Erie to the Hudson River twenty-five miles north of New York City. The Erie Railroad was in continual financial straits and quickly developed a reputation for a rough ride and rickety passenger cars.

House, a second rate Hotel where we sat with several others in a comfortless room, in which they built a fire in an open stove 'till 5 O'clock, when we breakfasted, & at 6 took the cars for New York.

This rail-road is noted for its grand & romantic scenery which embraces every variety from the loftiest hills, & steep ravines, to beautiful rivers & streams & flourishing towns & villages. Our course for some distance this morning followed the Alleghany [*sic*] River & was for the most part very high, continually looking down chasms & into pleasant valleys, bounded by high hills on the other side.

We dined at Elmira[7] on the Schuylkill River, which we afterward kept in sight for most of the afternoon. Afterwards the Delaware River until we could see no longer. Binghamton is one of the handsomest towns we saw & contains some fine mansions. Its population is about 5000. In one place the rail-road passed over a viaduct of several stone arches[8] with a deep valley below & a pretty village & near it a fine stone bridge over a wild ravine called the Cascade bridge. Both are in sight at the same time from one point of the road & with the high hills & deep precipices & valleys with woods & waters form a grandly romantic scene.

We stopped at a little place to get tea. I did not want any but Richard got some.

About 9 O'clock we changed cars at Sufferns[9] & arrived at Jersey City at a quarter past 12 O'clock at night. We crossed in the Ferry boat & reached 112 West Fourteenth Street about Two or just before, finding the servants waiting for us, as we had telegraphed from Elmira when we should arrive. Drank a hot cup of tea & went to bed, enjoying to the utmost a good, clean, comfortable bed once more.

---

7. Here Juliette wired home to announce their arrival. Ezra Cornell had built the telegraph line paralleling the Erie's tracks to help control the trains and manage freight.

8. One of the engineering marvels on the Erie line was the Starrucca Viaduct twelve hundred feet long built in 1847. The stone-arched viaduct soared one hundred feet over the valley.

9. Juliette and party left the train at Suffern to shortcut across New Jersey.

Epilogue

*J*uliette Starr Dana continued to live in New York City at 112 Fourteenth Street near Union Square. Before the Civil War her husband Richard remained abroad most of the time in China, India, the Middle East, and England. The family acquired a small farm called "The Pines" on the shore of a small lake in the Berkshire Hills of Massachusetts.

Young Richard and his mother remained close. As a remembrance of their 1852 tour he gave Juliette a copy of the 1855 first edition of Henry Wadsworth Longfellow's "Song of Hiawatha," a story based on Chippewa legends from Lake Superior, the northern big-sea-water Gitchee-Gumee. Richard attended Columbia College in New York and then entered the China trade at age twenty-one. He lived ten years in China and was the first western merchant to establish a trading post in the interior. Richard returned to New York in 1869, married Florine Turner, and fathered two boys. He built a home called Maple Farm, in Lenox, Massachusetts, and raised his family there and in New York. He continued to love horses and hunting all his life. Richard's health failed at the end of the century due largely to intestinal problems acquired in China. He died in New York in 1904 at age sixty-eight, outliving his mother by one year.

During the Civil War the Dana family had to sell "the Pines." Juliette's youngest son William graduated from the Naval Academy in 1863 and commanded a gun crew on Admiral Farragut's flagship during the battle of Mobile Bay. William went on to a career in the U.S. Navy and commanded several vessels before his death in Paris in 1890. Juliette's daughter Juliette Henrietta married West Point graduate General Egbert L. Viele, who had seen action in the

Mexican, Civil, and Indian wars. Viele later became a member of Congress and was chief engineer for New York's Central Park.

Juliette's husband retired from international trade in 1862, having circumnavigated the globe, it was said, fifteen times. Dana continued commercial and banking businesses in New York and became a governor of the New York Women's Hospital and a director of the New York Juvenile Asylum. Juliette and he lived together in New York the rest of their lives. Dana's eyesight gradually failed, and he died in 1894, eighty-two years old. After his death Juliette moved to Fifth Avenue and Eighty-sixth Street, living near her children. She died in New York City, January 23, 1903, at eighty-seven years of age.

Appendix

Juliette Starr Dana kept a detailed record of her expenses. This is her record:

Expenses of the Journey
For Two

	$ cts
Fare from New York to Albany	2 — 45
~~Apples & Crackers~~	" — ~~6 1/4~~
From Albany to Little Falls	3 — 30
Dinner at Little Falls	" — 75
To Newport by Stage	1 — "
Newport to Utica by Trenton falls	5 — 34
Dinner & Tea	2 — "
To Syracuse	2 — 12 1/2
From Syracuse to Auburn	1 — 30
In Syracuse for board	2 — "
For Omnibus	" — 25
From Auburn to Rochester	3 — 90
~~Refreshments & guide~~	" — ~~15~~
Hotel in Rochester	3 — "
Omnibus & Porter	" — 33 1/4
From Rochester to Lockport	2 — 45
~~Crackers & Apples~~	" — ~~8~~
At Eagle Hotel Lockport	1 — 34
Fare in stage to Youngstown	1 — "
Bill at Hotel	1 — 42

On Steamer Rochester for Lewiston	" — 50
Dinner at Lewiston	" — 50
Carriage to Clifton House	4 — 16
Chasm Tower, Devils Hole, & Whirlpool	1 — 50
	— 96
For seeing Museum & animals	" — 67
Expenses at Niagara	7 — 8
Fare to Buffalo	1 — 20
Fare to Detroit	10
	$59 — 92
Brought over	59 — 92
Carriage in Detroit	1 — 25
Bill at Biddle House	12 — 75
Fare to Mackinaw	4 — "
For taking care of baggage	" — 17
At Hotel Mackinaw	17 — "
For Porter	" — 11
Passage to Saut de St Marie	6 — 17
Hotel Saut Ste Marie	8 — "
Indian for Canoe	2 — "
Passage to Eagle Harbour	12 — "
Bill at Eagle river	15 — 50
Bill at Eagle Harbour	6 — 50
Waggon to the Mine	2 — "
R-s board one day	1 — "
Fare to Ontonagon & down to Saut	9 — "
R-s fare from Eagle Harbour	6 — "
Fare to Mackinaw	6 — "
At Mission house	10 — 16
Fare to Chicago	8 — "
Carriage at Milwaukee	1 — "
Porter—& boots	" — 42
Bill at Tremont house Chicago	5 — 50
Porterage	5 — 16
Fare Through to Galena with meals	16 — "
Hotel bill at Galena & porter	4 — 20
Fare to St Paul	6 — "
Board at St Paul	4 — "
Carriage	3 — 75

Board at St Anthony	3 — "
Fare on the Martha	10 — "
Bill at Dubuque	2 — "
Carriage	4 — "
	245 — 55

Bill at Galena	6 — 66
Porter	
Fare on Minnesota Steamer	14 — "
" —Flat-boat	1 — "
" Steamer Belle Gould	8 — "
Fare to Cincinnati	20 — "
Board & washing in St Louis	3 — 75
Carriage in St Louis	4 — 25
Porter	" — 25
Fare through to N. York	32 — "
Carriage, baggage, & porter	1 — 50
Breakfasts & dinners	2 — 50
Porter	" — 25
Porter & carriage	1 — 91
	96 — 7

Brought forward	245 — 62
	$341 — 62

Time—9 weeks 2 days

The expense of the above, was at the rate of *2 dollars* & *72 cents* per day *for one* $2.72

Selected Bibliography

The information in the Introduction and the footnotes was derived from a variety of the many publications readily available on American social and transportation history, Native Americans, major city histories, and military history. This selected bibliography includes sources that were available in the localities to which they relate. These include articles and reminiscences written in or about 1852, contemporary newspapers and magazines, various magazine articles and local histories, historical society and museum publications and files, the 1850 U.S. Census, directories, and encyclopedias. The Internet contains historical information and leads to many local sources.

Blegen, Theodore C. *Minnesota: A History of the State*. Minneapolis: University of Minnesota Press, 1975.

— "The 'Fashionable Tour' on the Upper Mississippi." *Minnesota History* 20 (December 1939): 377–96.

Bryant, William Cullen. *Letters of a Traveller*. New York: G. P. Putnam, 1850.

Carver, Jonathan. "Capt. Jonathan Carver, and his Explorations," *Collections of Minnesota Historical Society*. Vol. 1. St. Paul: Minnesota Historical Society, 1872. (A replication of the original parts issued in 1850–53 and 1856.)

Chaput, Donald. *The Cliff: America's First Great Copper Mine*. Kalamazoo, Mich.: Sequoia Press, 1971.

Dreyfus, Benjamin W. *The City Transformed: Railroads and Their Influence on the Growth of Chicago in the 1850's*. Accessed November 14, 1997 from http://homepage.interaccess.com/~dreyfus/history.html.

Dunlop, M. H. *Sixty Miles from Contentment: Traveling the Nineteenth-Century American Interior*. Boulder, Colo.: Westview Press, 1998.

Ellet, Charles. *The Mississippi and Ohio Rivers.* 1853. New York: Arno Press, 1970.

Ellet, Mrs. Elizabeth. *Summer Rambles in the West.* New York: J. C. Riker, 1853.

Fuller, George F. "Fort Snelling and Minnesota Territory." Ed. Bertha L. Heilbron. *Minnesota History* 29 (December 1948): 316–20.

Fuller, Margaret. "Summer on the Lakes 1843." In Mason Wade, ed. *The Writings of Margaret Fuller.* Clifton, N.J.: Augustus M. Kelley, 1973.

Harper's New Monthly Magazine. July 1850. "Scenes on the Erie."

Harper's New Monthly Magazine. July 1853. "Sketches on the Upper Mississippi."

Harper's New Monthly Magazine. February 1855. "United States Census of 1850."

Harper's New Monthly Magazine. December 1855. "Remembrances of the Mississippi."

Harper's New Monthly Magazine. March 1858. "The Upper Mississippi."

Harper's New Monthly Magazine. May 1866. "Galena and Its Lead Mines."

Heilbron, Bertha L., ed. *With Pen and Pencil on the Frontier in 1851: The Diary and Sketches of Frank Blackwell Mayer.* St. Paul: Minnesota Historical Society Press, 1986.

Howard, Edwin L., and Virginia M. Howard. The History of Youngstown. Lockport, N.Y.: Niagara Historical Society, 1951.

Hunter, Louis C. *Steamboats on the Western Rivers.* New York: Octagon Books, 1969.

Kaiser, Mrs. Charles A. *The Streets of Lockport: Notes on the Early History of the City.* Lockport, N.Y.: Niagara County Historical Society, 1948.

Kane, Grace Franks. "Recollections of Early Days at Mackinac." *Michigan History Magazine* 10. Lansing: Michigan Historical Commission, 1926.

Krause, David J. *The Making of a Mining District: Keweenaw Native Copper, 1500–1870.* Detroit: Wayne State University Press, 1992.

Lacy, Iblert, and Adelhide Z. Lacy. *Dusty Lockport Pages.* Lockport, N.Y.: Lockport Historical Society, no. 7., January 1952.

Lankton, Larry. *Beyond the Boundaries: Life and Landscape at the Lake Superior Copper Mines, 1840–1875.* New York: Oxford University Press, 1997.

Larsen, Arthur J., "Roads and Trails in the Minnesota Triangle, 1849–60." *Minnesota History* 11 (December 1930): 387–411.

Library of Congress. American Memory Historical Collections. Michigan Biographies. Searched on various dates 2002: http://memory.loc.gov/cgi-bin/query/.

Mackinaw Area Tourist Bureau. Mackinac Island Chamber of Commerce. Accessed July 2, 1997, from http://www.mackinawcity.com/planner/.

Macleod, William. *Harper's New York and Erie Rail-Road Guide Book.* New York: 1852.

Massie, Larry. "The Lights and Shades of the Reverend John Pitizel's Upper Peninsula Life." *Michigan History Magazine* 77, no. 3 (1993).

Minnesota Historical Society. *Historic Fort Snelling*. Accessed September 24, 1997, from http://www.mnhs.org/sites/snelling/.

— "History and Development of Great Lakes Water Craft" and "Vessel Types on the Great Lakes." Adapted from Labadie, Patrick, Brina J. Agranat, and Scott Anfinison, *Minnesota's Lake Superior Shipwrecks, A.D. 1650–1945*. Accessed February 10, 1998, from http://www.mnhs.org/prepast/mnshpo/ship/.

Monette, Clarence J. *The History of Eagle River Michigan*. Lake Linden, Mich.: N.p., 1978.

Morris, Lucy L. W., ed. 1914. *Old Rail Fence Corners, Frontier Tales Told by Minnesota Pioneers*. St. Paul: Minnesota Historical Society Press, 1976.

New York State Archives. *Guide to the Records of the Department of Correctional Services*. Accessed July 2, 1997, from http://unix6.nysed.gov/holding/aids/correct/intro.htm.

Peterson, Eugene P. *Mackinac Island: Its History in Pictures*. Mackinac Island, Mich.: Mackinac State Historic Parks, 1973.

Petersen, William J. *Steamboating on the Upper Mississippi*. 1937. New York: Dover Publications, 1995.

Roberts, Robert B. *Encyclopedia of Historic Forts*. New York: Macmillan, 1988.

Runge, Herman G., Collection. *Runge Vessel Index*. Milwaukee Public Library.

Rydholm, C. Fred. *Superior Heartland: A Backwoods History*. Vol. 1. Marquette, Mich.: C. Fred Rydholm, 1989.

Salt Institute. *History of Salt*. Accessed June 10, 1997, from http://www.saltinstitute.org/38.html.

Sedgewick, Catherine. "The Great Excursion to the Falls of St. Anthony." *Putnam's Monthly Magazine*. September 1854.

Seymour, E. S. *Sketches of Minnesota, the New England of the West*. New York: N.p., 1850.

Steele, Eliza R. *A Summer Journey in the West*. 1841. New York: Arno Press, 1975.

Steele, John. *The Traveler's Companion through the Interior*. Galena, Ill.: N.p., 1854.

Stone, Hon. J. W., *Address at the Dedication of Marquette County's New Courthouse, Marquette, Michigan, September 17, 1904*. Marquette, Mich.: Records of the Marquette County Clerk.

Swanholm, Mark, and Susan Zeik. *The Tonic of Wildness: The Golden Age of the "Fashionable Tour" on the Upper Mississippi*. St. Paul: Minnesota Historical Society Press, 1976.

Thurner, Arthur W. *Strangers and Sojourners: A History of Michigan's Keweenaw Peninsula*. Detroit: Wayne State University Press, 1994.

"The Tourist" for 1835, Pocket Manual for Travellers. New York: Harper & Bros., 1834.

Way, Frederick, Jr. *Way's Packet Directory, 1848–1983*. Athens: Ohio University Press.

Index